Love Affair

The Story of the Sirak Art Collection

To Helen
Best wishes.
Babette Sirak
12/20/91

by

Babette Sirak and Kirsten Chapman

Love Affair: The Story of the Sirak Art Collection

Published by the Columbus Museum of Art and
The Ohio State University with additional funding from
The Huntington National Bank

Editor
Elizabethe R. Kramer
Atticus Scribe

Graphic Design
Steven J. Sevell
Sevell + Sevell Inc.

Photography
Jeffrey A. Rycus
Rycus Associates Photography

Copy Editor
Margie Breckenridge

Copyright © 1991

LIBRARY OF CONGRESS CATALOG CARD NUMBER: 91-62770
ISBN: 0-918881-29-3

Printed in the United States of America

To Howard

Without whom there would be no story

Frontispiece
Our house on Commonwealth Park

Foreword

The history of collecting has always been an integral part of art historical inquiry. We in Columbus are remarkably fortunate to have witnessed the growth of a great art collection which, through the generosity of Howard and Babette Sirak, has long been made available, in its original setting at their home, to hundreds of scholars and students of the arts. We feel strongly that the human dimension of this collecting should be recorded. The best way to do this is through the personal voice of Babs Sirak herself. This is especially true now that the collection will be seen in the public space of the Columbus Museum of Art, where the individual works are recorded in a scholarly catalogue.

The Ohio State University, the College of the Arts, and the Department of History of Art have had a long and warm friendship with Howard and Babs Sirak. As medical resident, professor of surgery in the medical school, and then member of the Board of Trustees, Dr. Howard Sirak has been intimately involved in our university. Babs' relationship with the College of the Arts and the Department of History of Art has been one of sharing: She has given countless tours and study opportunities of their collection to our students and faculty during the last twenty years. In that same period, Babs has taken art history courses offered by our faculty— in particular, those of Professors Barbara Groseclose in American art and Francis Richardson in Italian Renaissance art.

Participation by The Ohio State University and the Columbus Museum of Art in the production of this unique book of paintings represents a further example not only of the collaborative spirit between our cultural institutions, but also of the rich artistic climate of Columbus.

—*Donald Harris*
  Dean, College of the Arts, The Ohio State University

Merribell Parsons
Director, Columbus Museum of Art, and
Adjunct Professor of Art History, The Ohio State University

Christine Verzar
Chair, Department of History of Art, The Ohio State University

Foreword

Art touches each of us in a different manner. It is a personal discovery of likes and dislikes. The Sirak Collection reflects the talents, determination, and tastes of two people captivated by art, its study, and its acquisition. *Love Affair: The Story of the Sirak Art Collection* is a very insightful and warm story that enables us to appreciate the Collection and its growth over the years. The anecdotes intimately share the love, commitment, and generosity of Howard and Babs Sirak to enrich others with their passion for art. Through it, we share the delight of their discoveries.

It is only natural for The Huntington National Bank to be a sponsor of this book in acknowledgment of our personal appreciation and relationship with Babs Sirak. As curator of The Huntington Collection, Babs' talents have not only beautified our work environment, they have also stimulated our employees' interests in art through docent training, art tours, artists' luncheons, and art appreciation courses.

Columbus is fortunate that Babs and Howard Sirak believed their exquisite Collection should remain intact and be available to our total community for generations to come.

— *Frank Wobst*
  Chairman and Chief Executive Officer
  Huntington Bancshares Incorporated

Acknowledgments

Special thanks to Christine Verzar, Chairman of the History of Art Department, The Ohio State University, who with her multiple skills and sheer willpower, played the lead in producing this book.

I am proud of my long association as art consultant to The Huntington National Bank, and with Frank Wobst, its Chairman and Chief Executive Officer.

Through imaginative leadership and generosity, The Huntington National Bank continues to enrich our community in many areas. I am grateful for its help in producing *Love Affair: The Story of the Sirak Art Collection.*

Finally, thanks to all those who have generously offered their gracious help: Margie Breckenridge, Michael Castranova, Stewart Curtis, Mary Ellison, Dan Fader, Sharon Ferguson, Don Harris, Elizabethe Kramer, Merribell Parsons, Norma Roberts, Jeff Rycus, Steve Sevell, the Sirak docents, Karen Updike, and Lois Foreman Wernet.

—**Babette Sirak**
  Columbus, Ohio
  June 1, 1991

Table of Contents

Prologue

Our son John began receiving his art education at the same time we did. He was two, and we were both forty-two.

In those days, Howard usually had to work at the hospital and didn't have much opportunity to see his youngest son. So we often put John between us in our bed. And, because we were looking at art books, he started to look at art books.

This went on for a couple of years. After a while, I began to notice that John had his own taste in art. Whereas we were looking mostly at Expressionism and Impressionism, he was attracted to the books illustrating contemporary art.

John particularly liked one book. I wish I could remember its name. It had to do with The School of Paris, but contained a lot of American painters as well. It was a big book and soon became his favorite. I spent a lot of time going through it with him and telling him the names of the painters. Instead of experiencing the child's world of "See, see, look, Jane," John looked at pictures by contemporary French and American artists.

From the beginning, he loved Arshile Gorky. Although Gorky was the first painter he really responded to, he grew to like a lot of the others as well. I began to notice that John would say a painter's name before I did when I turned the pages of that book. So, of course, I thought "Well, he's a smart little boy, but he's probably just memorized the order of the paintings in the book."

In 1966, when John was four, Howard and I took him to the Cleveland Museum of Art. He had never been there before. We entered the gallery containing the Winslow Homers and Thomas Eakins. John, bored, pulled at my hand. He wanted to move on. He broke away from me and ran into the next room.

Suddenly, we heard this little voice cry out in sheer delight, "Rothko!" John had spotted something by one of the painters he knew. Then he stood in the middle of the room and quickly pointed his finger at each painting, identifying every one by the artist's name. Although they were works of painters represented in the book I'd thought he'd memorized, this was the first time he'd ever seen these pictures. He hesitated at one painting and snapped his fingers, trying to remember. He turned to us for help and said, "Oh, you know I know this one; he's one of those hard-edged painters." It was an Ellsworth Kelly, we told him.

"Kelly!" he said. "That's right." And he went on and identified the last few.

The other people in the gallery, including a guard, were frozen as they watched our son. Moments afterward the guard came up to me and tapped me on the shoulder. "Madam, is he a midget?" he asked.

Almost in tears I answered, "No! He's just a little four-year-old boy!"

And everyone in the room went "Ahh!"

Of course, this was just fascinating to us. In fact, I take the blame (it wasn't Howard) for exploiting John. The minute an art magazine or some transparencies of paintings would come into the house, I would sit with John, and we would look at them. "Who painted this?" I'd ask him, and nine times out of ten he would know. John was identifying paintings like mad. This went on for quite a while.

Around this time, we loaned our Alexej Jawlensky to a large exhibition in New York. When the catalogue came, it contained black-and-white photographs of all the paintings. Because so many paintings were crowded onto each page, they were identified elsewhere. In the catalogue, I noticed that there was an early Gorky. The early Gorkys suggest Grant Wood's *American Gothic* in that they are paintings of his mother and father done as a bride and groom in the old country, standing very stiffly, the way the old couple does in Wood's painting. They actually have no more to do with the late Gorkys, which are abstracted shapes full of intense color, than *American Gothic* would have to do with Gorky.

On page one, in the midst of many other black-and-white photographs of paintings, was an early Gorky. I pointed to it and said, "John, who do you think painted that?"

He looked at it, and he said, "Oh, Gorky."

And then a chill went over me. I thought, "Oh, my God, what have we got here?"

That weekend, we went to a party where one of the guests was an old friend of ours, a wonderful child psychiatrist named Adolf Haas. I told Dr. Haas this story in hopes of an explanation.

"Why, it's very simple," he said. "John is four years old. His mind is uncluttered, and he really sees the essence of Gorky. You know, we adults have too much accumulated excess baggage that gets in the way of our perceptions." That was as good an explanation as I would ever hear for this particular phenomenon.

When John was five, and friends came to dinner, I would have him identify paintings in magazines. It was a parlor trick. I really was exploiting him by then. One day, *Art News* arrived, and on the cover was a Jackson Pollock.

"John, come here," I said. "Look, here's one of your favorite artists. Tell me, who painted this?" There was silence.

Then John looked up and stared me right in the eye. "I don't know," he said.

"Oh, John," I countered. "This is easy. You know this one. Come on, tell me who painted it."

Again he looked me squarely in the eye, and in a very firm voice he said, "Mom, I don't know." Then I realized that he had stopped playing the game. He was finished. He was through with me. He was not going to be exploited anymore.

Years later, when John was a senior in high school and always short of money, he and his dad and I were

" Suddenly, we heard this little voice cry out in sheer delight, 'Rothko!'"

seated at the dining room table reminiscing about his childhood adventure with art.

I said, "John, I bet that now you can't even name the paintings in this house."

"Oh, I bet I could," he said. "How much do you want to bet?"

I felt very sure of myself. "OK," I said, pointing to *The Gypsy Girl*, by Renoir, "I'll give you $100 if you can name the artist who did the painting that's in the corner of this dining room."

His face became beet red. "I know, I know, I know," he cried. And he jumped up and down.

My heart started sinking. I asked, "Well, who is it?"

"It starts with an R," he said. "Rembrandt!" he cried triumphantly.

When I told him he was wrong, he insisted that I immediately take him around the house and reintroduce him to each and every painting in our collection.

Introduction to the Tour

People often ask, "How did you get started collecting?" I must answer truthfully that the whole thing was by chance. Howard and I were married in 1961. One day, three years later, we were in New York, walking along 57th Street. We came across a place called Knoedler's, one of the best art galleries in the city. Though my father was not a collector, he had bought a painting there fourteen years before. Howard and I had never been inside a commercial gallery. So I said, "Let's go in here." And we walked inside.

An elegant salesman named Martin Jennings came up and asked if he could help us. We said we were just looking, but before we knew it we found ourselves up on the fourth floor viewing art. An assistant kept carrying out paintings, one after the other, to display them. Then, Martin closed the velvet drapes. It was pitch black except for the light above a large easel. We saw one by Maria Elena Vieira da Silva that we liked very much. Next we saw this absolutely smashing painting, much bolder, much more expensive and totally different, by Emil Nolde, called *Sunflowers in the Windstorm*. But soon we had to leave to catch a plane and couldn't decide which painting to take—if any. Then Martin Jennings uttered the legendary lines that Howard loves to repeat. "We'll ship it out at our expense. You can live with the painting for a month or two. If at the end you decide you don't like it, ship it back at our expense. You see—it really won't cost you a cent."

Howard and I looked at each other, and one of us said, "Wow, this is a great deal."

We had a big house with lots of empty walls. After a short discussion, we decided to have the Vieira da Silva shipped to us. When it arrived, we put it in the living room, and it looked wonderful there. Then we put it in the dining room, and it looked wonderful there. It looked wonderful wherever we tried it. At the end of two months, we didn't send the da Silva back. Instead, Howard sent a check.

In the meantime, I committed the fatal deed. I bought an art book on Emil Nolde and his German Expressionist friends. We had no idea who Nolde was. We often studied the book in bed with John, our two-year-old son, between us. John was raised on art.

And that's how we started. We loved looking at art books. I went to the libraries and took out every art book I could find. That fed our desire to learn more and more.

We didn't get back to New York for six months. This time, instead of accidentally wandering into Knoedler's, we hastened to its door. We were ushered to the fourth floor and again shown the Nolde. We again received the same assurances from Martin Jennings, how it wasn't going to cost us a cent. The painting was sent to us, and we lived with it for nearly three months. Finally we realized we couldn't live without it. Once more, Howard sent a check.

We became more and more involved, subscribing to art magazines and traveling to museums, where we began looking at paintings critically. We sought out examples of great works of art. We tried to determine why they were considered great, why they had lasted through the ages, while others hadn't. When we were alone, we spent all our spare time thinking and learning about art. It was really a love affair between Howard and me and between us and art. As you continue the tour, you'll notice that I use the word "love" a lot because we really do love our paintings. It's not a word I use lightly.

After we bought the Nolde, we went crazy. That's the only way to describe it. By the end of the first year, 1965, which was the year after we bought the Vieira da Silva and the Nolde, we had acquired thirty-six works of art.[1]

I still have my day-to-day calendar from 1965, and I can't figure out when we had time to do all this. Howard was a busy heart surgeon. We had seven children. I was active in

[1]Vlamnick, Utrillo, Monet, Müller, Klimt (two), Soutine (two), Gleizes (two), Delaunay, Schiele, Kirchner (three), Jawlensky, Severini, Klee (six), Beckmann, Bissier (two), de Staël, Derain (two), Feininger, and another Nolde, as well as some other paintings we eventually sold.

community things, and I was a room mother for at least two of the children's schools. My parents were still alive, and they and other members of my family lived here in Columbus. Besides all this, we were responsible for the care of our large home. But I always say that the house had a lot to do with our continuing to buy art. It had so many empty walls that it always accepted more and more paintings.

We have often thought that if we had owned a different house, we probably would have stopped buying paintings much sooner because we wouldn't have had the space. And we never bought for investment or for any reason other than we loved a particular work and wanted to live with it. There was nothing in the closet.

Home, family, and career kept us tied to Columbus. Only infrequently did Howard and I escape to New York City. Once there, from Friday morning when we arrived until late Sunday afternoon, we turned into "Babs and Howard—art people." It was during this time that we had the great fortune to meet Ulfert Wilke and Sam Salz, two individuals who were to play invaluable roles in our new adventure.

We were introduced to Ulfert Wilke on a sunny Sunday morning. Our good Columbus friends Dixie and Tony Miller had asked us to join them at Dick Zeisler's apartment in New York City. We enjoyed meeting Dick and seeing his fine collection. But the best thing that happened that morning was meeting Dick's friend Ulfert Wilke. He was a charming man, born in Germany.

Ulfert was timeless. He was eternally young, eternally curious. A director for many museums, he was a teacher, sculptor, and painter. But most of all, he was an avid collector. He collected antiquities. He had built up large collections of American Indian art, African art, Etruscan art, Persian plates, and God knows what else. Ulfert kept a daily journal of all his activities, which he maintained his entire life. He didn't earn very much, but the minute he had his hands on a couple of hundred dollars he would buy something for one of his collections. In those days—the '50s through the '60s—you could do that. Some things were more expensive, but nothing like the prices a decade later. Ulfert also traded with dealers and other collectors. He reveled in that.

"In the meantime, I committed the fatal deed."

When we left Dick Zeisler's apartment that Sunday afternoon, Ulfert came along and spent the rest of the day with us. After dinner, we went back to his apartment, where he showed us some of the objects he had collected. By the time we departed, we felt a real relationship with him had begun. Indeed it had. It lasted until the day he died, at the age of eighty-two, in 1988. Ulfert was a very important person in our life. He opened doors for us. He knew practically everybody in the art world, and everyone knew him. He introduced us to private collectors and to reliable dealers. He let us know when he encountered exceptional paintings at a gallery.

It was through Ulfert that we bought our Etruscan pottery. In 1966, he came to visit us in Columbus. Several of our new paintings hung in the living room. Walking about, Ulfert suddenly spied the shelves near the end of the room, full of wedding presents.

"How can you have bric-a-brac in the same room with these fine works of art?" he demanded.

"But Ulfert," I said, "this is all we have."

He thought for a minute and said, "Lend me your car tomorrow, and you won't be sorry."

When I returned home late in the afternoon the next day, I found our shelves had been transformed. The wedding presents had disappeared. Sitting on the second shelf were three black, mysteriously beautiful Etruscan pots, made in Italy around 800 B.C.

Ulfert had driven to the Dayton Art Institute, where his Etruscan collection was being shown, to inform his friend Tom Colt, the director, that he was "borrowing" three of his own pieces. Back at our house, he carefully packed all the wedding gifts and put them away in the attic.

A year later Howard said, "Babs, we've got to reimburse Ulfert for the pots or send them back." Over the years we ended up buying his entire collection. We have since been told that we have one of the biggest private Etruscan pottery collections in the United States. We owe it all to Ulfert.

— 🐞 —

We first learned of Sam Salz through a man who was known as a "runner"[2] in the New York art world. (At that point, Howard and I owned only the Vieira da Silva and the Nolde.) The runner was arrogant. In the course of a conversation, he asked us if we knew Sam Salz. "No," we said.

"Well, how can you call yourselves collectors if you don't know Sam Salz?" he said disdainfully.

"In the first place," Howard answered, "we don't call ourselves collectors. We've bought a couple of paintings, that's all. There's a lot we don't know. Who is Sam Salz?"

"He's a great Impressionist dealer in New York. But of course he would never be interested in people like you. He deals only with the Mellons and the Rockefellers and the Fords. Also, he's inaccessible and temperamental."

That's all Howard needed to hear. The next time we were East, we decided to try to get in touch with this inaccessible, temperamental Sam Salz. I told Howard, "I'm sure he'll have an unlisted number." But I was wrong—it was right in the New York phone book.

Howard called and said, "Hello, my name is Howard Sirak. I'm a doctor from Columbus, Ohio. My wife and I have bought two paintings. We're just trying to learn, and we hear that you're very knowledgeable and that you have beautiful paintings. We'd like to meet you."

Sam replied, "So how about tomorrow morning at 11:00?"

We went to his seven-storied private house at 7 East 76th street. When you walked into

---

[2]A middleman who takes paintings on consignment.

The eternally young, eternally curious Ulfert Wilke

Sam Salz, a work of art himself

Sam's—if you were an art person—it was as if you had died and gone to heaven. His home was beautifully furnished, full of exquisite paintings and Chinese bronzes. That's how we met him. That's how inaccessible and temperamental he was. That's how we got into Impressionism.

Sam didn't have a gallery. As a matter of fact, he never thought of himself as a dealer (he hated dealers). He just thought of himself as having this beautiful collection of paintings that he would sell—*"Boite Postale"* (Mail Box), he often called himself.

Sam was born in Vienna in 1894. When he was a young man, he went to Paris to try to earn his living as a painter. He became friends with many of the artists in the painters' quarters: Modigliani, Picasso, Soutine, Bonnard, and Vuillard. He kept comparing their work to his. He noted that people bought his friends' pictures but not his, so he became a dealer instead. In the beginning, he approached his fellow painters saying, "May I try to sell one of your paintings? If I do, you'll pay me a commission?" They agreed because they were having difficulty selling their work themselves.

Eventually he met the Durand-Ruel family. At least six decades earlier, members of this French family had been dealers for Monet, Renoir, Pissarro, Cézanne, Sisley, Degas, and others. By the mid-20th century, the family (which, according to Sam, had seven different branches) had become enormously wealthy. In 1950, Sam was named executor of their paintings. He advised them to put one-half of their holdings in Switzerland. He foresaw the day France might begin to preempt the paintings to keep them from leaving the country, which is, indeed, what happened. Soon thereafter, France passed a law that prohibited the exportation of objects considered to be national treasures.

The family Durand-Ruel followed his advice and acquired a vault in the basement of a large bank in Geneva. Sam shrewdly rented a vault across the way. Every once in a while Sam pried a painting out of them. There would be a transfer from their vault to his. Some of the paintings in our collection came out of Sam's vault. Many others came directly from the Durand-Ruel family or relatives of the artists. Because the paintings had so few previous owners

" Ulfert Wilke and Sam Salz were to play invaluable roles in our new adventure."

and hadn't been publicly displayed, Sam referred to them as his "virgins."

When Sam came to the United States in 1939, he took a suite at the Ambassador Hotel in New York. He brought with him more than 160 paintings by Monet, Pissarro, Renoir, Cezanne, Sisley, Degas, Manet, Soutine, Matisse, Bonnard, Vuillard, Toulouse-Lautrec, Van Gogh, Gauguin, and many others. He sold to private collectors, many of whom ultimately bequeathed their paintings to museums.

Occasionally, on a rainy day, Sam, Howard, and I would go to the Metropolitan Museum and wander through their Impressionist collection. Sam would point out those pictures he had sold, recounting to whom he had sold them and at what prices. Sam's earlier decision to give up his career as a painter in order to sell the paintings of others was fortunate for American culture. In his lifetime, he was responsible for bringing thousands of great paintings, sculptures, and drawings to this country.

When it comes to art, I've always thought of Sam as the head of an orphanage, where every child was precious. He wanted to make sure his children were placed in good homes. He didn't care if a customer did not buy one of his paintings; eventually, the right person would. In fact, people virtually stood in line for the chance to acquire one of his paintings. So it was just a question of whom Sam fancied. Fortunately for Howard and me, he grew very fond of us.

The first time we went to Europe, Sam met us in Paris, where we spent a week together. A couple of other times, we joined him on the Riviera. He even came to Columbus. He adored my mother and father. He loved me as well, but Howard, in a way, became like a son to him. I think in us he finally found some people who understood what he was about, people who truly appreciated him and the art he loved so much. A complex person, Sam Salz was a work of art himself.

Tour With Anecdotes

In one of the attic rooms, Howard has a large office where he keeps our extensive library of art books and catalogues. There is a big file of media articles and a special folder containing hundreds of thank-you letters from people who have toured the collection. I've included a couple of examples on the following pages.

These tours began in 1966 and continued right up until early 1991, when the collection was transferred to the Columbus Museum. During those 25 years, thousands of people came to our home to view the collection. I led most of the tours myself, except when the groups were too large; then Howard and I each would take half. After 1983, tours also were given by the specially trained Sirak docents from the museum.

The tours were comprised of a great diversity of people—practically every organization in town, public and private schools, colleges, universities, volunteer groups, business and professional people, art groups, artists—all received a tour on request. People came from all over the Midwest and, later, from all over the United States, Europe, and the Far East. I guided museum directors and curators, National Endowment for the Arts people, and most every celebrity who came to town.

We had a particularly close relationship with The Ohio State University. For nine years, Howard was a university trustee, and in the late '70s, I began studying art there with Babs Groseclose, who soon began bringing her classes to our home on a regular basis. This practice was adopted by other colleges and universities.

And last, but certainly not least, family, friends, friends of friends, and children of friends came to visit the collection.

In spite of the sometimes arduous schedule of touring, I enjoyed it because I felt that I always received something back from my "captive audience."

May 21, 1989

Dear Mrs. Sirak,

The highlight of our "marvelous *two* days in May" was seeing your collection, and having you guide us with your wonderful commentary not only regarding the works, but the artists, and the periods in their careers which the paintings represent. Your own experience in searching and studying made the tour very intimate and special. I kept wishing I could have it all on tape.

I find myself going through your home again with you and trying to remember. I hope the Columbus Art Museum will have a catalogue prepared someday.

Having the art shown in a home makes it so special—that's why I love our Taft Museum, the Frick and others of this kind.

Thank you for sharing your collection and your time.

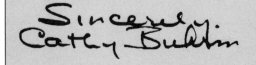

Sincerely,
Cathy Bulkin

June 5, 1974

Dear Babs and Howard,

Thank you very much for your thoughtfulness in sending us "Private Faces, Public Places." It is a delightfully easy companion and fun to escape into.

My operation was preceded a couple of weeks earlier by a biopsy, so my last two visits to you and your paintings came during the time of heightened sensitivity that a first square look at mortality forces upon one. I hope you can imagine what it meant to me to share Howard's guided tour with my friends and to store away all that artistic joy for use in coming days. I even had an inward chuckle about your Ensor when I was waiting in the operating room.

So you see, I'm more grateful to you than I can say.

Affectionately,

Jean

" Our collection was a private affair, and maybe that's what people realized when they came to see and share it with us."

Frequently, I would be given a fresh insight into a particular work of art by one of their observations. I often regretted that because of the touring group's tight schedule I was unable to become better acquainted with so many stimulating people.

I suppose you could say that Howard and I bent over backward to receive people in our home. To our parents, who brought us up to share, belongs the credit for our "open door policy."

I think what people responded to was the opportunity to see paintings of this quality in a home where a family actually lives. In a way, our collection was a private affair, and maybe that's what people realized when they came to see and share it with us.

Join me now as I begin the final tour of our collection while it still hangs in the house on Commonwealth.

Howard's Dressing Room

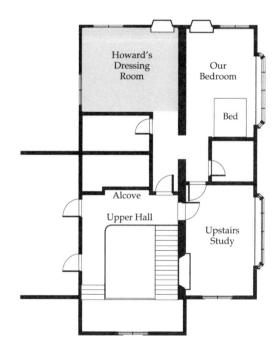

Howard's Dressing Room

Our Bedroom

Bed

Alcove

Upper Hall

Upstairs Study

The Atlantic, which hangs above the sofa, is the first painting that we purchased. It was painted in 1961 by the Portuguese artist Vieira da Silva. Her works are held by many major museums.

This painting was executed later than any of the others that are going to the museum. Studying it, you can visualize forms of buildings, bridges, and docks. It's a view of a coastal city, perhaps Marseilles. At the time we bought *The Atlantic*, in 1964, it was a contemporary work of art. As you'll soon discover, we went backward in time in our buying. It wasn't done on purpose; it's just where life led us.

In the corner of this room is a little Vlaminck. Here, I'll put the light on so you can see it better. This is called *Field of Wheat*. It's the third painting we acquired. We love it not only for itself, but also because the man from whom we bought it inadvertently led us to Sam Salz.

All the other works in the room were done by André Dunoyer de Segonzac. Segonzac, who lived to be ninety-three, was and still is enormously popular in France. Sam always used to say that the reason he wasn't better known in America was that it was too difficult for all of us to pronounce his name.[3] This oil painting, *Notre-Dame de Paris*, was done in 1913. You have to move away from it to see it properly. I love that muted-color palette. It's a powerful painting. It was in the Segonzac retrospective show held at the Louvre at the time of his death.

Because he and Sam Salz were best friends, we had the opportunity to meet Segonzac at lunch in Paris in 1967. Sam was the host. The guests were Howard, myself, Segonzac and his wife. She was an aging actress from the Comédie Française. In those days, I was wearing my hair in a French twist, the way it appears in my portrait bust by Jack Greaves. Segonzac was studying me the way a painter does, and suddenly he said, *"Tiens! Vous-vous ressemblez Nefertiti."*

I knew enough French to know what that meant. "Well, thank you!" I said. "That's so nice." I patted him, and he patted me. After lunch, Howard and I went out to look at museums (that was about all we were doing on that trip), and when we got back to the hotel there was a beautiful art book of Segonzac's work. Accompanying it was a note on the back of a famous art postcard dated September 2, 1967 (and I translate): *"Dear Madam, I send you these modest images of Queen Nefertiti, your cousin of more than three thousand years ago for which it tells you how much my wife and I have been enchanted by knowing you and also the doctor, thanks to our friend Sam Salz."*

There are several stories related to the *Notre Dame* painting. The one I like best concerns a visit to an auction preview at Parke Bernet.[4] (We liked auction previews because they were a great way to learn.) We recounted to Sam how bad the works looked. Some of the paintings were so soiled, you could hardly see them.

A few days later, after we'd returned to Columbus, Sam went to the Parke Bernet preview. With his eagle eye, he spotted a filthy painting on the floor. Realizing that it was one of the great early oils by Segonzac and that it had been lost for a long time, Sam did further research in his library back home. When the day of the auction came, Sam instructed his secretary, who was new, to go to the auction and bid on this picture.

"But, Mr. Salz, I have never been to an auction," she said. "I wouldn't know what to do. How do I do it?"

"Just keep bidding until you have bought it— just keep putting up your hand." Then he cautioned her, "Don't tell anyone where you're from until after you've won the bid." Had it been known that Sam was eager to buy it, the price would have soared.

The secretary succeeded in buying the painting inexpensively. After the bidding, she was approached by an auction representative, who asked, "Madame, how shall I bill you?"

---

[3] It's pronounced *se gón zak*.
[4] This was before Parke Bernet was bought by Sothebys.

Howard's Dressing Room
Our first painting: *The Atlantic* by Vieira da Silva

Howard's Dressing Room
Notre-Dame de Paris by de Segonzac

"Oh, just send the bill to Mr. Sam Salz," she said, much to his astonishment. Everybody turned around and stared.

We next saw Segonzac's *Notre Dame* on an easel in Sam's house. It looked fabulous. He merely had had it cleaned. We immediately bought the painting from him. Sam put a Louis XVI frame on it—the only Louis XVI frame in the collection. But then, every painting that came from Sam Salz was placed in a carefully chosen antique frame. He believed that a great painting deserved a great frame.

When we returned home, Howard wrote to Segonzac, telling him that we had acquired his painting. André wrote back saying he was thrilled to know of its current whereabouts. It had been in the collection of John Quinn, a lawyer from Tiffin, Ohio, who had been a true patron of the arts. He had subsidized the publication of *Ulysses* by James Joyce, was involved with the Irish Abbey Theater, and was instrumental in promoting Irish poets and painters in the United States. An avid collector, he had built a fantastic art collection. Quinn helped get legislation passed that eliminated import duties on fine art—a most important accomplishment for the development of American museums. A bachelor, he died suddenly. Because he left no will, his collection was put up for auction.

In 1978, the Hirshorn Museum in Washington held an exhibition of some of the former Quinn paintings, including our *Notre Dame*. It was exciting to see part of his collection reassembled, but I was sad to see a notice at the end of the show asking for information concerning the whereabouts of many of his pictures that remained "lost." This had a powerful effect on me. Somehow we would have to find a way to keep our collection together.

" Somehow we would have to find a way to keep our collection together."

Our Bedroom

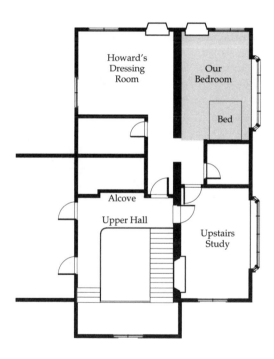

Let's go into our bedroom. The painting right in front of you, over the fireplace, is *Sunflowers in the Windstorm*, by Emile Nolde. Howard refers to this painting as the "fatal peanut" because as you know, it is the one that put us into high gear studying art. Take yourself back in time, and try to see it through our eyes—the eyes of absolute novices. This was a very bold painting for us to buy in 1964, at the beginning of our collection. We had never heard of Emil Nolde, and we knew nothing about German Expressionism. But now we realize that this one painting represents the characteristics associated with German Expressionism. Bigger than life, the flowers suggest three people struggling to withstand the storm. They burst out of the canvas. The deep purple color of the sky is in the artist's mind rather than an imitation of nature. The painting seethes with movement and emotion.

Eventually we bought these two watercolors by Nolde. As you go around the house, you'll realize that this was to become our pattern. If we liked an artist and could find other good examples of his work, we would try to buy them. The watercolor *Steamboat and Sailboat* was done in 1913. *Young Girl* was painted around 1905-1906, while *Sunflowers* was done in 1943.

The big painting over my bureau was painted in 1920 by Lyonel Feininger. At that time, he was teaching at the Bauhaus, along with Klee and a wonderful group of artists who remained together for a short period of time. The Bauhaus lasted as long as the Weimar Republic, 1918 to 1933. Our painting is called *Cathedral*. We always thought we were fortunate to get this rare, wonderful Feininger, and we've never seen one that we like better. Our theory is that the circular motif denotes the ringing of the church bells. Feininger scholars who have seen our collection believe this is the only painting in which he used circles, perhaps influenced by his knowledge of work by Robert Delaunay. Later, in the hall, you will see the circular patterns in our two Delaunays. This influence of one painter on another is typical of the many connections you will find in our collection.

We bought *Cathedral* from Greta Feigl. She was the widow of a dealer in New York who had come to the United States before World War II, bringing many paintings with him. The former owners to whom her husband had sold *Cathedral* returned it to her on consignment for resale. We had bought a painting from her, and she knew that we were interested in a great Feininger. One Sunday while we were in New York, Greta Feigl called us at our hotel to tell us she had found a fabulous Feininger. Having just bought a painting from Sam, Howard told her that he wasn't sure we were in the market for another, but we would come over.

On the way to the airport, we stopped at her apartment. Before we went upstairs, we made a pledge to each other that we weren't going to buy another painting that weekend, no matter how good it was. We had reached our limit. We even kissed over this pledge. We went upstairs, and there was that damn painting. It was so-o-o beautiful. Howard and I looked at each other and knew that we would not be able to keep our pledge. We agreed to buy it.

Over our bed is the poignant self-portrait of Ernst Ludwig Kirchner. It's called *Tower Room, Fehmarn (Self-Portrait with Erna)*. Though he and Erna never married, she was always with him. The painting depicts their favorite retreat overlooking the Baltic Sea. Done in 1913, the year before World War I started, Kirchner was at the height of his power. He had been the leading painter of Die Brücke (the Bridge). The next year he had to join the German army. After a nervous breakdown, he returned to Germany. Eventually he and Erna went to Switzerland, where some years later he killed himself.

So there he is, in his tower room—young and at his artistic pinnacle. I think this picture is so wonderful because he strove to isolate himself and Erna in that space. It emphasizes the great intimacy between them. He is doing a sculpture of her, while over her shoulder through the window, one sees a sailboat on the Baltic Sea. In the foreground, a pale green shawl is draped over the chair.

Our Bedroom—View from Our Bed
Sunflowers in the Windstorm by Nolde (the "fatal peanut")
Cathedral by Feininger

Next to the *Tower Room*, on the right, is a surprising earlier painting by Kirchner, called *Girl Asleep*. It is reminiscent of the way the Fauves were painting at this time, in 1905. If you search the canvas carefully, you will find at the bottom an "E.L.K. 1901." It's likely Kirchner inscribed this over the original paint—an obvious attempt to make it seem as though he had invented the Fauve movement. An art historian named Donald Gordon wrote a book about Kirchner in which he used both of these pictures. He believed that *Girl Asleep* actually was done in 1905 or 1906, not in 1901.

This little painting on the left is by Jan Müller. Müller was an American of German descent. He was born in 1922 and died in 1958 of valvular heart disease. He was said to have been a wonderful man, much loved by other painters. He was fascinated by Shakespeare and Goethe. Our picture is called *Apparition from Hamlet*. Over the years, I've developed my own theories about what he is trying to say. In Shakespeare's play, Hamlet picks up Yorick's skull and says, "Alas, poor Yorick, I knew him, Horatio." Those faces behind him represent the ghosts of Polonius, Laertes, and others whom he killed, who now haunt him. I think that's certainly Hamlet with Yorick's skull, and I believe the weird figure in the front on all fours is Hamlet's passive self, the part of him that couldn't make up his mind. It's a great theory, but I'll never know because I can't ask Müller. The manner in which the artist depicted the trees and the setting is typical of his Teutonic scenes. He also did paintings that were just abstractions of color. But he died young, so we have no way of knowing how he would have resolved his two styles.

The other two works, on the closet doors, are drawings by Gustav Klimt. This is one of his famous subjects. It is called *The Embrace*. I've often thought the man's chin reveals his vulnerability. Klimt was a wonderful draftsman. With only a few beautiful lines, he could convey much passion. His other drawing is of Mrs. Adele Bloch-Bauer, a society lady whom he painted many times. I love her hauteur, and her little string purse. We learned about Klimt in 1965 when we attended the Guggenheim Museum's Klimt and Egon Schiele exhibition. Howard and I were impressed by what we saw, and we set out to search the New York galleries. We soon learned that none of the great oils by Klimt and Schiele were available, but

"We never bought a picture because of the artist's name."

eventually we found very good drawings by both of them.

I want to digress a moment to emphasize an important point about our collecting credo: We never bought a picture because of the artist's name—we sought only top-quality examples of the artists whose work we loved.

As we walk into the study, please notice the watercolor by Feininger hanging on our bedroom door. It's called *Ship in Distress*. It shows Feininger's humor and love of architectural lines.

Our Bedroom
The Embrace by Klimt

Our Bedroom — Over Our Bed
Tower Room, Fehmarn (Self-Portrait with Erna) by Kirchner
Girl Asleep by Kirchner
Apparition From Hamlet by Müller

The Upstairs Study

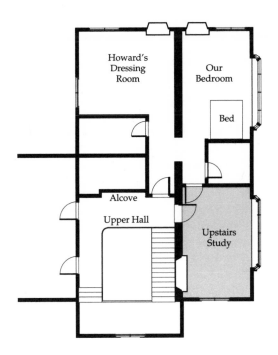

We've often called our upstairs study "the Klee Room." One day, during that frenetic year of 1965, Howard and I were in Staempfli's, a gallery in New York, when we spied *Ilfenburg* by Klee, hanging on a back wall. We were immediately drawn to it and bought it. We knew nothing about Paul Klee, so we did our customary thing: We bought books to inform ourselves about him. Because Klee was a prolific writer, and others have written so much about him, we developed an extensive Klee library. Eventually, we acquired ten more works by Klee.[5] If you study the late paintings, you will note that his images, due to his failing health, are much less refined. Although child-like in their execution, they remain powerful.

The other Klee paintings hanging on the wall with *Ilfenburg* (1935) come from various periods of his artistic life. The painting at the top, *Fire-Spirit (Feuer-geist)*, was done the year before his death in 1940. He was suffering from a rare, incurable, crippling disease called scleroderma. This picture reflects his premonition of death—his depiction resembles a death mask.

Through Ulfert Wilke we met a man named Fred Schang. He was an impresario, and, like Sol Hurok, he managed artists. Every day, when he walked to his office in Carnegie Hall, Schang passed a particular gallery. In the window he kept seeing a little drawing of a woman's face. She was like a young, quixotic-looking Greta Garbo. Gradually Schang fell in love with the woman in this drawing by an artist whom he'd never heard of, Paul Klee. He bought the drawing and wound up becoming an avid Klee collector, eventually owning nearly 100 of his works.

At the time we met Schang, he was starting to sell some Klees because he wanted to form a trust for his grandchildren. He sold us *View of Saint Germain*. It came from Klee's sketchbook that he did in Tunis in 1914 while there with August Macke, a young artist who later was killed in World War I. At that point, Klee didn't know if he was going to be a professional musician (he was an excellent violinist), a teacher, a writer, or a painter. After his visit in Tunis, he wrote in his diary, *"Now I know I want to be a painter!"*

With the Yellow Half-moon and Blue Star (1917) also was bought from Fred. He told a wonderful story about this picture. In 1922, in the days of the Bauhaus, where Klee was teaching and painting, the winter was severe. Everybody was poor except an American girl studying there. One of the other students asked whether she would be willing to do her a favor.

"Professor Klee is having a hard time making it through the winter, but he is a very proud man," the student said. "Do you think you could get $200 from your father? If you could, I would select some of his work for you to buy."

The American student loved her teacher and his work, so her father sent the money. Her German friend went to Klee and picked out eight pieces. The pictures were carefully wrapped and given to the American. It turned out that the German girl was Galka Scheyer, who later amassed a great collection of Klee's work.

Thirty years passed. The American, now living in Louisville, Kentucky, went up to her attic one day and rummaged through an old trunk. Inside, she found a roll of brown paper. She couldn't remember what it was, so she unwrapped it. There, in pristine condition, were the Klees. She called a dealer in New York, asking if he wished to buy eight Klees painted during the Bauhaus period. The dealer hopped on the next plane to Louisville and snatched them up. Because Fred Schang had been such a good customer, the dealer offered him first choice. Schang chose *With the Yellow Half-moon and Blue Star*.

Thoughtful (1928). Fred Schang told us he used to identify with this painting. He thought the worried man could have been a portrait of himself.

---

[5]On this last tour, as in all the others, there is never enough time to discuss in depth all eleven Paul Klees, but I always identify them by name and date.

Upstairs Study
"The Klee Room" (see key on next page)

1. *With the Yellow Half-moon and Blue Star*
2. *View of Saint Germain*
3. *Ilfenburg*
4. *Lonely Flower*
5. *Thoughtful*
6. *Fire Spirit*
7. *City between Realms*
8. *usque ad finem* (by Bissier)
9. *A.31.Oct.62* (by Bissier)

Lonely Flower (1934). As in so many Klees, the natural form becomes almost human. To me, this flower with its lovely ribbons of color is a shy, introverted person who literally is tied up in knots.

City between Realms (1921). This is our only watercolor where Klee also used black oil transfer. His humor, whimsy, and unique imagination are clearly revealed.

Let's examine *Rock Flower* (1932), another watercolor by Klee, which hangs over the big brown chair. *Rock Flower* uses the same beautiful pastel hues that you saw in *Lonely Flower*, but this image is more abstracted with its irregular lines. In surprising contrast appears the funny little face of a spirit.

Now let's look at *Dream of a Fight* (1924), a drawing by Klee. It appears as if a lightning bolt is striking a knight and his companion, causing them to come apart. For a long time after we bought this drawing, I would smile to myself every time someone said, "I just fell apart." I would always visualize this drawing—limbs, body, everything—all coming apart at once.

Now I'm standing in front of the two Klee oils. Ulfert had seen this painting in Germany. He cabled Howard to say there was a wonderful Klee that might be for sale, but a German museum was interested in it. Were we? Howard said we would be interested in seeing it, but we wouldn't buy sight unseen. Could it be shipped over? It arrived, and much to our amazement, on the back of this painting, called *Still Life with Dove* (1931), there was another painting. Both works were done on a board much like masonite. The board needed to be cradled (which requires gluing strips of wood to the back of the board to flatten it) because it was beginning to buckle. But this cradling or bracing would have destroyed the second picture. Instead, we had a conservator split the board, thus producing two paintings. It took him many months. Finally, near Christmas, we received a call. "Merry Christmas!" we heard. "You now have two Klees!"

The second painting, *Composition* (1931) was titled by the Swiss dealer Ernst Beyeler.

One night, after we had lived with these two pictures for eight years, I sat on the couch looking at them while talking to my daughter Nancy. All of a sudden, I saw a connection between them. It appeared to me

> " *As in so many Klees, the natural form becomes almost human.*"

that *Composition* had been an outline for the much more complex *Still Life with Dove*. If you compare the two paintings, *Composition* has the same line of the table found in *Still Life with Dove*, but the line also is part of a bird. If you use your imagination, *Composition* could be an abstract bird. The big green circles appear in both paintings.

I have my own thoughts about the similarity in the way the paintings are shaded. Perhaps Klee was exhausted after painting *Still Life with Dove*, which required a very difficult, encaustic[6] technique to express his complicated, Cubistic-like method of painting. I can just see him finally finishing this painting and thinking, "Oh, my God, there must be an easier way to do this," flipping over the board and whipping off *Composition*. Of course, as Howard pointed out, it could have been the other way around. *Composition* could have been a blueprint for the more complicated painting. There is, of course, the third possibility—that the two had no relationship whatever.

Now we're looking at two paintings by James Ensor: *The Assassination* (1890) and *The Sea Shells* (1895). Some well-known art expert once said facetiously that we had the biggest private collection of Ensors in the United States—two!

One day we were going down in the elevator with Sam after looking at paintings in his fourth-floor viewing room. I mentioned that Howard and I were reading an interesting book about Ensor. Sam's face lit up. "You like Ensor?" he asked.

"We've only seen his paintings in books," I said. "But we think he's fabulous."

Sam immediately pressed the stop button, and back up to the fourth floor we went. "Come with me," he said, leading us toward the large storage closet. (Howard always offered to help carry out the pictures, hoping that he would get a chance to see what was in there, but Sam would never allow it.) Sam reached inside and pulled out the painting called *The Assassination* and leaned it against the closet door. I remem-

ber my first impression of the painting, especially the marvelous reds. They were the richest reds I'd ever seen.

"Oh, Sam, it's just beautiful!" we cried.

We didn't even ask each other. We started grabbing each other's hands, and Howard asked, "Would that ever be for sale?"

Sam replied, "If you really love it, you can buy it." So we had it sent home. I remember my dad's first reaction to the painting. He hated it. He couldn't understand how anyone would want to live with that painting. In fact, he stated that living with it might be considered a punishment. On the other hand, my mother adored it. I have since found, from my numerous tours, that this work is a litmus test. Strong women have always liked it.

Ensor was born in 1860 in Ostend, Belgium. By studying the painting, you can see that he was troubled. As a young man, he was a lonely, unhappy person, but it was during this period that he did his greatest work. He hated his parents, and he especially hated doctors. We particularly enjoyed the irony of Howard, the heart surgeon, owning this picture. By the time Ensor was forty, his parents had died. He had become famous and happy. He had acquired a mistress and traveled extensively. But, on the whole, he had deteriorated into a mediocre artist!

We learned about the location of the second Ensor, *The Sea Shells*, as a result of Howard's reading about the first one in Haesaerts' book on Ensor. He noticed that Sam Salz was listed as the owner of both pictures, although Sam had made no mention of it at the time we bought the first one. Howard telephoned Sam and asked if, indeed, he still had the seashell painting. Sam admitted that he did. The next time we visited him in New York, he had it hanging on the wall in his back living room.

I must tell you how we felt when we first gazed upon *The Sea Shells (Les Coquillages)*.

[6]A painting process in which colored beeswax is applied and fixed with heat.

Upstairs Study
Still-Life With Dove by Klee

Upstairs Study
Composition by Klee

The first time I looked at this painting, I thought, "Oh, isn't it beautiful!" After further study, I found myself shuddering because there is something sinister about it. The thought flashed through my mind that this may be the way the world would look if a nuclear bomb exploded. Everything is destroyed except for some lonely bit of beach where only the inanimate remains. This reaction is enhanced by a sky that is empty and cold. In our later reading, we learned that Ensor worshipped J.M.W. Turner, one of England's greatest landscape and seascape painters. Once you know this, you can see that his sky is much influenced by that artist.

Ensor has given the seashells in this painting a life of their own. The seashell on the top forms the apex of a pyramid and conveys the impression of a strong, dominant male. The seashell to its lower left appears to be looking up at the male symbol and seems, with its pinkness, to suggest a soft, pleading female. If you continue studying some of the other shells in the painting, you will see masklike, unfriendly faces. They make me feel a little paranoid.

If you turn back to *The Assassination (L'Assassinat)* and look at the faces staring through the windows, the faces of the puppets, the faces on the clothing on some of the puppets, and the face of death, you will begin to appreciate how obsessed Ensor was with these images. I think his obsession culminated in his most famous painting, *Christ's Entry into Brussels* (now at the Getty Museum), which is covered with hundreds of faces, including the artist's.

I want to add a few more words about Ensor's *The Sea Shells*. For a long time after we bought the picture, it hung at the end of the living room. When we first put it there, we thought it would live harmoniously with the Impressionist paintings. But for some strange reason, *The Sea Shells* conveyed a totally different mood, jarring the entire room.

In 1977, the purchase of our last great painting occasioned an extensive rearrangement of the collection. *The Sea Shells* was brought upstairs to hang with *The Assassination* and the Klees. For some inexplicable reason, the Klees and the Ensors hung together beautifully and contentedly. Even though you probably don't think of them as spiritual cohorts, they must be. Also, I must add that the little Bissiers, which have hung quietly for so many years just catty-

"Some well-known art expert once said facetiously that we had the biggest private collection of Ensors in the United States—two!"

corner to the wall of Klees, have really held their own.

I don't know much about Bissier. We heard about him through our friend Ulfert Wilke, who knew Madame Bissier. And we bought these paintings early, in 1965, the same year as Bissier's death. They're enigmatic little works.

There's a story I enjoy about Bissier, who, like Klee, lived in Switzerland. In 1969, Igor Stravinsky came to Columbus to conduct our symphony. This was, of course, a thrilling time for local music lovers. The head of our orchestra then was Evan Whallon. Jean, his wife, loved music and also loved our paintings. She often came to our home. One day, she called and excitedly asked if she could bring out Madame Stravinsky, who had accompanied her husband to town. Madame Stravinsky loved paintings, Jean said, and had a collection of her own.

As Howard and I showed Madame Stravinsky around the house, she was appreciative and polite, but very cool. She didn't seem to be responding to what she saw. This surprised us. When we walked into our study, she looked at the Klees, but then suddenly spotted the Bissiers. "Bissier!" she cried. "You have Bissier! Oh, I love Bissier!" She had known him and owned some of his paintings. Madame Stravinsky then changed completely. She became very warm and friendly and open. She told us how wonderful our paintings were. By the time she and Jean left, it was as though we were good friends. Every time I think of Bissier, I recall Madame Stravinsky's exclaiming, "Bissier, oh, Bissier!"

A similar experience occurred with Arnoldo Pommodoro, the well-known Italian sculptor, who was in town for a large show of his works at the Columbus Museum. During his stay, he and his dealers and some museum people came to the house to see our collection. As soon as he saw that we had two Medardo Rossos, a Morandi, and a Severini (all Italian artists), he had the same reaction as Madame Stravinsky. Suddenly, in his eyes, we were accepted as people of taste!

Upstairs Study
The Assassination by Ensor
The Sea Shells by Ensor
Rock Flower by Klee

The
Upper Hall

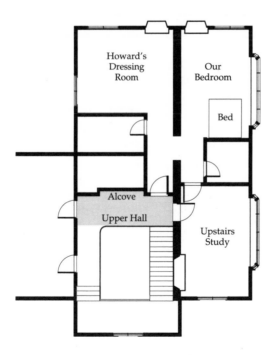

Here in the hall is *Schokko with Red Hat* by Alexej von Jawlensky, done in 1909 or 1910. Jawlensky was born in Russia but spent most of his life in Germany. He often exhibited with Kardinsky, Klee, and Feininger. They called themselves "The Blue Four" and were promoted by Galka Scheyer.[7] Jawlensky was influenced by Matisse's famous portrait of his wife, *Woman with a Hat* (1905), completed a few years earlier when Jawlensky spent time in Matisse's studio. To me, this painting is almost like a Russian icon, reflecting the artist's Russian soul. I especially like its title. "Schokko," German slang for "chocolate," was the model's nickname because she was always eating it

We bought *Schokko* from a dealer named Leonard Hutton. We had to wait to see if we *could* buy it because the Guggenheim Museum had the right of first refusal. The Guggenheim people were debating between this Jawlensky and another, larger painting of a lady wearing a turban. That one was a bit more expensive, but we thought *Schokko* was the better Jawlensky and the one we really wanted.

One day Leonard called to tell us that the Guggenheim had bought the other work. We were delighted, and *Schokko* came to us.

Once the painting arrived, we found it so powerful that we struggled to find an appropriate place to display it. We first tried to hang it in the dining room opposite the Nolde *Sunflowers*. That didn't work. They warred with one another, upsetting the tranquility of our dinner hour. Then we tried to put *Schokko* in the living room, but she overpowered the other paintings. Howard and I even went outside and looked at her through the French doors. From that vantage point, we could almost, but not quite, tolerate her. One night, we had a brainstorm and hung Schokko here in the hallway alcove, where she presides in splendid isolation. I'll be interested to see how the museum handles the placement of her.

[7]We met her on page 20 when she was a student at the Bauhaus.

Turning to the left, you will see the *To Jacques Nayral*, by Albert Gleizes. Gleizes often is referred to as the intellectual of the Cubist movement. I don't know how well he'd like that title. I'm sure he would prefer to be called one of the best painters in the Cubist movement. To my mind, he wasn't one of the best, but at times he was wonderful. We think that in this particular painting, a portrait of a man he really loved and for whom he mourned, Gleizes was at the top of his form.

The man is Jacques Nayral, the artist's brother-in-law and best friend. The picture, painted in 1917, is dedicated to him. The big "7" that runs through the center of the painting tells you that this was the year Jacques Nayral was killed in World War I. The "86" in the painting stands for Nayral's infantry number. As in many other Cubist portraits, this one is probably full of clues—some that we can only guess, some that we think we understand, and some that we'll never understand. Nayral's profile becomes the figure "4," referring to 1914, when World War I started. Howard and I have always been sure that Nayral was a musician because there are musical notations in this painting. Look at his ear, and you will see that it resembles a musical note.

A story I like to tell about this painting concerns the famous European sculptor Jean Tinguely, who visited Columbus some years ago. He came to the house one day to see the collection. When he discovered this painting, he exclaimed, "Tiens! Gleizes!" And then he added, "I didn't know he could paint so well."

The first time we saw this painting was in 1965 at the Columbus Gallery of Art, as it was then called. *Jacques Nayral* was part of a traveling Gleizes show that had been organized by the Guggenheim. Howard and I were attracted to the painting and went to view it many times. We learned it belonged to the dealer Leonard Hutton, and that it was for sale. Howard agreed over the telephone to buy it when it finished its exhibition run ten months later in New York. When we finally went to see the painting there, we were thrilled to discover that we still loved it. Later, we bought another

Upper Hall
Schokko with Red Hat (presiding in "splendid isolation") by Jawlensky

Upper Hall
To Jacques Nayral by Gleizes

Gleizes, a much bigger one, which we hung down in the front hall where the de Staël is now. It was a large, colorful painting, and we had it for about two years. But then, as Howard said, we'd "come to the end of it." There was no mystery left, and so we sold it.

Perhaps some of you are wondering how many other pictures met a similar fate. Over the years, we've sold eight paintings, perhaps ten percent of the works we bought. Our only test was living with them and seeing how well they survived among the other works of art. Fortunately, we made our mistakes early on.

For example, the sixth painting we bought was a large Vlaminck, about three by four feet. We hung it in the dining room, and at first we thought it was wonderful. Sometime later, Howard and I were taking a walk, and we both started talking at once. "Do you really like the Vlaminck as much as before?" he asked.

"That's so funny," I answered. "I was just going to ask you the same thing."

That very night, we went back and looked at it together. All of a sudden we hated it. Howard took it off the wall, wrapped it up, and put it away in the attic. Many months later, we sold it at auction. In those days prices weren't rising rapidly, but we got our money back, plus a few dollars.

We had the same reaction to a Modigliani that we had enjoyed for several years. It hung in our library, but when it began to wear thin, we sold it at auction, much to the consternation of some of our friends. When we realized we never missed it, we were confirmed in our judgment. Gertrude Stein had a great line about this: "When a painting begins to fade into the wall, then it's time to sell it and let somebody else enjoy it."

As I mentioned, this phenomenon of a painting falling out of favor happened to us a few times. Interestingly, it would always occur to both of us at the same time. Howard and I have very different personalities, but we always agreed on art. I've often said that had we fought about what we wanted to buy, we wouldn't have pursued our collecting. We never bought a painting that we both didn't love. We learned to turn pictures down, and we never hesitated to send things

" Howard and I have very different personalities, but we always agreed on art."

back after living with them for a short while if we didn't think they met that criterion.

I'm looking at Schiele's *The Thinker (Self-Portrait)*, 1914. Egon Schiele was probably one of the most tragic figures in art. In his short and stormy lifetime, he suffered all kinds of sorrow. Though he lived to be only 28, he managed to produce 3,000 works. He and his wife and their unborn child died in the flu epidemic of 1918 that swept over Europe and the United States. Schiele was obsessed with a presentiment of death and sex. He was always poor. I believe he went to prison because of the subject of some of his drawings: nude young girls. Even in this drawing, *The Thinker (Self-Portrait)*, there's a premonition of death. The head is almost like a skull, and yet, compared to other Schiele portraits, it's really quite mild.

Now about the Max Beckmann. This painting, called *Two Negroes in a Cabaret* (1946), is set in a nightclub. In the upper part of the painting, you can see a leg of a woman sitting on a higher level. A railing separates her from the two men, who are sitting holding drinks, but who appear lonely and alienated in their environment. What can be more lonely than to be strangers in a strange place? Beside them is this mysterious totem figure. Who is she? A waitress? I don't think so. I think she is an imaginative figure representing their homeland or whatever it is they're missing. To me, it's also a painting of black and white colors that you can read, the way you would calligraphy.

This painting is particularly meaningful to us because it once belonged to our friend Ulfert Wilke. He first saw it when he was in Beckmann's studio. The painting was propped up against a wall. On each visit, Ulfert would admire it. One day Beckmann said, "Ulfert, why don't you buy this painting?"

And Ulfert replied, "Because I don't have any money."

"Well, it's a painter's painting," Beckmann said, "so pay me what you can, when you can." Delighted, Ulfert accepted the painting.

He told me that for a long time he made payments of small amounts to Beckmann. This continued until one day Beckmann finally said, "Ulfert, you've paid enough."

That first time we met Ulfert, we saw the Beckmann hanging on his apartment wall on the west side of New York. A few months later, we bought it.

We now are looking at two Delaunays. The larger of the two, *Portuguese Woman* (1916), was owned by a famous French art dealer named Louis Carré. After we were shown a transparency of it by Martin Jennings at Knoedler's (who at the time had a connection with Carré), we indicated an interest in the picture. Knoedler's had it sent to us from Paris. One day, a huge crate arrived at our back door. Howard removed the slats from the box, and gorgeous color began to emerge. I was jumping up and down with excitement like a little kid. Howard said something to this effect: "Well, I can see you're going to be a great help in negotiating the price." I had seen only a portion of the painting, but I already had fallen madly in love with its seductive color.

Delaunay and his wife, Sonia, were primarily interested in color and the relationship of colors to one another. They headed a movement called Orphism, in which different colors were expressed as a circular motif. In *Portuguese Woman*, you can see an interesting connection to Klee. Klee first met Delaunay in Paris in 1912. That same year, he also translated one of Delaunay's essays on light and color. I am especially reminded of Klee when I look at the upper right-hand portion of *Portuguese Woman* because there are some of those beautiful pastel shades that Klee used so well.

The other Delaunay, *Air, Iron, and Water*, was done twenty years later for the Paris Exposition of 1937. Here Delaunay refers to the air age, the steam engine, and, of course, his beloved Eiffel Tower. He put the Eiffel Tower in his paintings whenever he possibly could, and often, I believe, in paintings where it didn't really belong. I've always assumed that the river is the Seine. In the front, you see the

Upper Hall
The Thinker (Self-Portrait) by Schiele

Upstairs Landing
Two Negroes in a Cabaret by Beckmann

Upper Hall
Portuguese Woman by Delaunay
Air, Iron, and Water by Delaunay
The Old Ladies (sculpture) by Jack Greaves

Three Graces, who probably represent his homage to the arts. Done in 1937, the painting is most optimistic, considering what was to happen two years later to France and to the rest of Europe.

Hanging next to the Schiele is Kirchner's *Landscape at Fehmarn with Nudes (Five Bathers at Fehmarn)*. This is one of those paintings we acquired in that frenetic year of 1965. We bought it from Greta Feigl, who was, as you will remember, the woman from whom we bought our Feininger. Howard has an amusing name for this painting; he calls it "The Poor Man's Cézanne." Cézanne's influence on Kirchner is clearly visible, as it can be seen in the works of so many young painters who flocked to Paris in 1906 during the great Cézanne retrospective. It had a profound effect on the whole history of modern art. Cézanne was, without a doubt, a seminal influence. Although *Bathers at Fehmarn* is very much influenced by Cézanne, it is also very much Kirchner. His *Tower Room, Fehmarn (Self-Portrait with Erna)*, which you saw in our bedroom, was painted in Fehmarn, too.

We have two Derains done during the Fauve period. The first, *Portrait of Maud Walter*, is the portrait of a famous French collector, named Maud Walter, who eventually left her great collection to the Louvre. I remember the first time that I saw this painting, I thought it was of a young man. It turned out to be Maud Walter when she was a young woman. This was painted in early 1905, just as Derain was becoming committed to the Fauve style. *Portrait of Maud Walter* has had an unusual role in our house because it has always been our night light. The light above it is always on when we go to bed. When we come home after having been out for the evening, the Derain is there to greet us. One of the nice things it's done is illuminate the sculpture *The Old Ladies* by Jack Greaves, which sits on the landing. The lighting enables you to see it through the windows from the outside. We've always joked about its visibility because if you didn't know that these old ladies were a sculpture, and you looked up casually as you walked by, you might think there were two people sitting in the window, guarding our home.

"Portrait of Maud Walter has had an unusual role in our house because it has always been our night light."

Upper Hall
Landscape at Fehmarn with Nudes (Five Bathers at Fehmarn) by Kirchner

Downstairs Front Hall

Now we're down in the front hall looking at two Soutines. The way we discovered Soutine was typical of how we learned about art and artists. In 1965, we visited the Barnes Museum in Merion, Pennsylvania, near Philadelphia. Among all the other treasures, we saw a lot of Soutines. We had never heard of him before, but we liked him a lot.

On our next visit to New York, we went to Knoedler's and asked if they had a Soutine. Indeed, they had this exciting painting, the one on the left, called *Landscape at Cagnes* (1923). Three years after we bought it, we went to Haut-de-Cagnes, a French village overlooking the Mediterranean, and discovered that the painting was much closer to reality than we had imagined. Haut-de-Cagnes is an old town where you can see the remains of a leaning, slanting wall built by the Romans. The balconies of the houses jut way out, providing a beautiful view of the sea. Soutine and, for a short time, Modigliani, lived and worked here.

Hanging next to it is Soutine's earlier landscape, done in the Pyrenees, called *Landscape at Céret*. Soutine had gone to Céret immediately after his great friend Modigliani died. The day after the death, Modigliani's mistress, Jean Herbertine, who was pregnant with their child, killed herself. Suddenly, Soutine's two best friends were gone. There is a story that he was so distressed, he wanted to blot out all memories of this period. Before he would sell one of his later pictures, he required the buyer to find a canvas from his earlier Céret period and bring it to him. Soutine would then destroy it, reimburse the client, and sell him a picture of a later period. Perhaps the artist was ashamed that the Céret paintings revealed too much of his inner, emotional self.

Chaim Soutine came from a wretchedly poor, Lithuanian Jewish family. His father was a cobbler and wanted Chaim to follow in his footsteps, but Soutine rebelled and walked to Paris—more than 1,000 miles from his hometown! Among all the artists we have represented in this house, Soutine was what you might call a natural painter, one who painted by the seat of his pants. By going to the Louvre and studying the great artists, especially Rembrandt, he taught himself how to paint without any formal instruction. Sam Salz knew Soutine very well and tried to bring him over to this country just before the outbreak of World War II. He even bought him a ticket to accompany him to New York. The day the ship was scheduled to depart, Soutine arrived at the dock and told Sam, "I just can't leave France." Sam never saw him again.

Head of a Young Woman (1901) is a sculpture by Medardo Rosso, who died in 1928. We learned about him through our friend Jack Greaves, the sculptor. When Jack was in Rome on a sculpture scholarship, he learned to love Rosso. Rosso is a sculptor's sculptor. Few people outside Italy, even those who know art, are familiar with this artist. This may be because Medardo Rosso did very few bronzes. Most of his work was done in wax over plaster because, as the story goes, he was too poor to afford bronze. Actually he preferred wax because of the translucent qualities and the suggested lack of permanence. He had a great influence on modern Italian sculpture. He and Rodin knew one another, and there has been a lot written about who influenced whom. The answer depends on which monograph you read.

Here in the corner is a charcoal drawing by Henri Matisse, called *Maternity*. It was done in 1939, when Matisse was sixty-nine. Over the chest is a painting by van Dongen, *Lilacs with Cup of Milk* (1909). Van Dongen usually painted women. He *loved* women. One of the clues to the authorship of this picture is the use of green on the woman's hand. This is a color he often used. Our friend Ulfert Wilke speculated that perhaps this painting was commissioned for the entrance hall of a grand house in Paris.

The lilacs are so sensuous. Howard thinks van Dongen painted them almost as though they were women's breasts because the blossoms are so full and hang against gravity. After we bought this painting from Sam, I couldn't wait until the lilacs bloomed in our backyard. I

Downstairs Front Hall
Landscape at Cagnes by Soutine
Landscape at Céret by Soutine

wanted to arrange some in a vase and place them next to the painting. I was amazed to see that the blossoms didn't even resemble those in the painting. But that's artistic license.

The upper part of the painting, with its beautiful circles of color, reminds me of Delaunay, who in 1909 was immersed in totally abstract color painting. It strongly suggests cross-fertilization between the two artists. Over the years, we've been intrigued by the critical placement of the white highlight on the front of the blue vase. If it weren't there, and the vase were a solid blue, the painting wouldn't be half as exciting.

During this period, van Dongen was living at the Bateau-Lavoir with Picasso. Both, along with Braque and Matisse, were being bought by the two great Russian collectors Shchukin and Morozov. In the fall of 1990, Howard and I made a thrilling discovery when we visited the Hermitage in Leningrad. We saw five van Dongen paintings of great quality. They covered an entire wall. The only other artist represented in that spectacular room was Matisse.

This next work, by Edouard Vuillard, is a pastel called *The Big Tree (The Tree Trunk)*, 1930. It shows what a great artist can do with the simplest of subjects. I love to look at it when I first come in the front door because the farther away you are, the better you're able to appreciate the roundness of the tree.

This painting was in Vuillard's family, the Pierre Roussels,[8] whom we met through Sam Salz. We once had dinner in their house with Sam, who was a close friend of theirs. The painting had hung in their dining room. In those days, Sam would sit opposite it and yearn for it with his eyes. One day, the family surrendered and sold it to him.

On the opposite wall is a work by Nicolas de Staël entitled *The Volume of Things (Volume des Choses)*, 1949. This de Staël and the Vieira da Silva upstairs are the only nonrepresentational paintings we have in the collection.

De Staël was born in Russia in 1914, but when he was a baby, his parents, White Russian emigres, fled to Paris. In 1954, when he was only forty years old, de

" [The Big Tree] shows what a great artist can do with the simplest of subjects."

---

[8]Pierre Roussel's father was Jacques Roussel. Pierre's grandfather was the French painter K.X. Roussel, whose wife was Vuillard's sister.

Staël, a manic depressive, committed suicide by jumping from the third-floor balcony of his home.

Oddly enough, the author Somerset Maugham played a part in our buying this unusual painting. Back in 1965, we received a catalogue for an auction preview to be held at Parke Bernet. While leafing through it, we were struck by a Matisse painting of a woman with a green parasol. It had been in the Somerset Maugham collection.

We went to New York to view the Matisse but were diverted by this much more beautiful, large abstract painting. After we returned to Columbus, Howard measured the wall here in the front hall to make sure the de Staël would fit. He called Coe Kerr, president of Knoedler's, and asked him to bid on our behalf. A few nights later, Coe called us from the auction and said, "You've got your painting."

Literally, *The Volume of Things* is a *heavy* impasto painting done on wood. The day we hung it, Howard asked that I help lift it onto the hook: "You take one side, and I'll take the other." I could barely lift my side.

At that time, the Monet with trees and shadows, which you'll see in the dining room, was hanging in our living room above the fireplace. You could stand in the front hall and see both the de Staël and the Monet at the same time. The day after our new painting was hung, that's exactly what I did. I spent hours looking at the two of them. When Howard got home from the hospital, I said, "You know, I think there's a connection between Monet and de Staël. I don't know what it is, but I think it's there."

He countered, "I don't see it." A couple of days later, some friends sent us a book on de Staël. I turned immediately to the part about 1949 and came across this glorious sentence: "In 1949 de Staël came under the influence of Claude Monet." I couldn't wait for Howard to get home.

View of the Front Hall
Lilacs with Cup of Milk by van Dongen
The Big Tree (The Tree Trunk) by Vuillard
The Volume of Things by de Staël
Head of a Young Woman by Rosso

The Library

Now that we're in the library, let's look first at Monet's *Basket of Grapes* (1884). This is such a luscious little painting. A lot of people, when they first see it, think it was done by Bonnard. Sam Salz used to talk about the "continué" in art—how an artist picks up something from a predecessor and adapts it to his or her own style or mode of expression. This is present in all the arts and, indeed, in all of life. I think this is a wonderful example of the "continué" because you can see Monet's influence on Bonnard.

Howard and I have always admired the significant role Monet's signature plays in this picture. His choice of red and its placement in the upper left-hand corner are so important to the balance of the composition.

As you look around the room, you'll see three still lifes: one by Monet, one by Morandi, and over the fireplace, the mysterious early painting by Matisse. Monet's is the earliest one, and yet it's the most free, the most modern. In 1975, this was one of two Monets we loaned to the Chicago Art Institute's Monet show. A year before, we lent *Basket of Grapes* to the Carnegie Museum in Pittsburgh for a show called *Celebration*. A Pittsburgh couple had seen *Basket of Grapes* in that show, and earlier in our home, while touring with a group from the museum.

A few months after the Monet show opened in Chicago, I received this letter from the couple: *"We just had to let you know that we attended the Monet Show in Chicago. While in the exhibit, which was enormously crowded, we finally reached [The]* Basket of Grapes. *We overheard the couple in front of us admiring the painting. The man turned to his wife and said, 'Now there is my favorite painting in the whole show.'"*

The letter continued: *"My husband and I were so proud. We looked on it as our painting, too."*

Below the Monet is our other Medardo Rosso. This is called *Sick Boy*. I once read that the artist visited a hospital ward, where he saw a little boy. He was touched by something in the

youngster's face, and he went home and did several versions of this sick child.

At a Brancusi show at the Guggenheim, Howard and I noticed the tremendous influence of Medardo Rosso on the early Brancusis. Here is a very *direct* influence because, if you ignore the boy's features and observe the egg-shape of his head, you will see the foreshadowing of Brancusi's later famous pure style. Here again is the "continué" in art.

In the front of the room is a little Renoir which looks a lot like a Monet. It's *The Bay of Naples* (1882), depicting in the background Mt. Vesuvius on a quiet day. This painting is much more beautiful in the late afternoon when the sun comes through the windows. The natural light makes the pastel blues just sing.

Hanging catty-corner to the Renoir is a portrait of a man called Thadée Natanson. It's an early Bonnard. Bonnard, Vuillard, and Félix Vallotton had helped form the Nabis, a group interested in exploring the use of flat pattern in their painting. *Portrait of Thadée Natanson* is dedicated by the artist to his subject: *"In remembrance of the summer, 1897."* It was during that summer that Vuillard and Bonnard visited the Natansons.

Madame Natanson, who was called Misia, later became a famous femme fatale. Both Vuillard and Bonnard were captivated and inspired by her. Among her many "activities," she was instrumental in getting Les Ballets Russes started in Paris.

I once asked Sam, "Why in the painting does Thadée's left hand look almost like a paw?" He explained that Thadée was a great talker; he was left-handed and gesticulated a lot when he spoke. Sam thought Bonnard was making a little comment on that habit.

Recently Arlene Weiss, a Sirak docent, was standing in this exact spot in front of Thadée. The painting is one that she loves very much, so she took extra care in describing all of its characteristics and history. She sensed that one woman, who was staring at her, was listening very hard. Finally Arlene said, "Are there any questions?"

Right away the woman nodded her head. Arlene waited expectantly. "Where did you get your shoes?" the woman asked.

On the other side of the window is Morandi's *Still Life* of 1945. Once he began painting still lifes of bottles, jars, and vases, he devoted the rest of his life to them. He would rearrange them for different paintings and at times, paint decorations on their surfaces. Morandi found a magical world within these still lifes. I think he is an artist quietly coming into his own.

In 1965, the year Morandi died, Howard and I bought a book about him because his paintings were unfamiliar to us. After studying him, we fell in love with his work. We searched many New York galleries, but we couldn't find any of his pictures. People rarely want to sell them because they are such rewarding works to live with. We did hear about a man in Italy who had more than ninety Morandis, but even he wouldn't sell any. Then we mentioned our interest to several dealers. A few years later, a Morandi finally surfaced in Switzerland. The dealer flew all the way from Europe to Columbus with *Still Life*. He went back to Europe without it.

Alongside the fireplace is our only Cézanne, *Seated Bather* (ca. 1873-1877). It has an interesting provenance. Cézanne's dealer, Ambroise Vollard, a good friend of Sam Salz's, had bought it from Cézanne. After Vollard's death, Sam bought it from the estate. *Seated Bather* used to hang in Sam's bedroom, where he had a lot of other beautiful works. Howard and I would gravitate to the Cézanne and stand there, looking at it longingly. Sam had a pet phrase: "I've taken to a decision." We learned to listen very attentively when he said that. One day he uttered this phrase and then said that we could buy the Cézanne. This was his habit—he would *allow* us to buy something. We carefully wrapped it in a little sack and headed from Sam's house on East 76th Street back to our room in the Sherry Netherlands Hotel at 58th and 5th Avenue. We often had walked those twelve blocks, but this time it felt as though we were flying. You won't believe what we did next.

It was late afternoon, and we had a date for dinner and the theatre. We propped up the Cézanne on the

"We propped up the Cézanne on the hotel dresser facing our bed."

hotel dresser facing our bed, so that when we returned that night, it would be there to greet us. Can you imagine doing that today? The next morning, we put it back in the paper bag and carried it with us on the plane to Columbus.

Over the fireplace hangs a painting that has caused museum directors a lot of embarrassment when they try to identify it. We love to play guessing games with them, and only rarely are they able to name the artist. This is an early Matisse, painted in 1896, when he was only twenty-six years old. It's called *Still Life with Self-Portrait*. It is fascinating to know he had been painting for only six years. It is especially fascinating to look at the complexity of this painting and see what he already had achieved artistically. To me, it demonstrates his incredible talent. When he was twenty, Matisse worked as a law clerk and hated it. When he became ill with appendicitis, his mother, just to amuse him, brought him some paints. Her simple gift changed modern art history. Matisse never went back to the law firm.

In this early painting, the artist appears to have been much influenced by Chardin, but there is also influence from the Dutch still-life painters who preceded him. This picture is really a tour de force because Matisse appears deliberately to have given himself a very difficult challenge: In the background, he includes the tapestry, and in the foreground, books and objects on the table that either tumble out or recede from the viewer. He beautifully incorporates high tones with a subdued palette.

Next to the Matisse is a painting by Odilon Redon. He was a friend and contemporary of the Impressionists, but he himself was not an Impressionist painter. This painting is very atypical because when most people think of Redon, they visualize beautiful flowers or weird faces like those in his prints done in homage to Edgar Allen Poe. In this painting, called *The Two Graces* (ca. 1900), his use of gold paint harks back to Medieval art. I love those arms linking the two women together. My father used to say that it reminded him of the Bible story of Ruth, when she says to her mother-in-law, "Whither thou goest, I go..."

After we had acquired this picture from Sam Salz, Ulfert Wilke came to visit us. This painting is so unusual that Ulfert had to study it for a long time to guess who painted it. Finally, he muttered, "Hmmm, I think Redon."

And I said, "You're right— now how did you arrive at that?"

"Only by the red, by the little red petals in the foreground. That was my only clue," he replied.

Library
Basket of Grapes by Monet
Sick Boy (sculpture) by Rosso

Library
Portrait of Thadée Natanson by Bonnard

Library
Still Life by Morandi

Library
Seated Bather by Cézanne
Still Life with Self-Portait by Matisse
The Two Graces by Redon

The Dining Room

Let's move into the dining room. We have wonderful light in here this morning. I'll still turn on the picture lights, but I love to see the paintings in the natural daylight. This Monet, *View of Bennecourt* (1887), and the Utrillo in the living room were the first two paintings we bought from Sam Salz the weekend we met him. Bennecourt is a small town on the Seine. People who have been there say it remains pretty much unchanged. You can see the church and the town through the trees. However, the most wonderful thing in this painting is Monet's bold handling—bold for 1887—of the trees and the shadows that appear black but, on close inspection, really are not.

Catty-corner to the Monet is our third painting by Chaim Soutine, *Melanie The Schoolteacher* (ca. 1922). I've often thought that Melanie looks as though she has had a hard life but somehow has survived. Note the delicate painting of her neck and face contrasted with those large, expressive, working-class hands.

As I mentioned before, Soutine was so poor that when he left Lithuania, he walked all the way to Paris. He made his way to Montmartre, the artists' quarter, where he met Modigliani.

In the early 1920s, Dr. Albert Barnes,[9] the Argyrol[10] King, went to Paris to buy art. He saw a painting in a little Montmartre shop window. He went inside and asked who had painted it. The owner told him it was by that "crazy painter Soutine who lives upstairs." Dr. Barnes climbed the steps and bought out the studio. He purchased nearly 200 pictures very cheaply. It was the making of Soutine. To celebrate, he took a taxi from Paris to Nice.

Renoir's *The Gypsy Girl* is charcoal with pastel highlights on canvas. Howard and I have always felt that Renoir really loved this picture and spent a lot of time on it. He even colored her. In natural light, you can see the color he has added to her hair, face, and arms. There's even blue in the background. This pastel was

done in 1879, a few years before *The Bay of Naples*. It shows Renoir's great skill as a draftsman.

Over the fireplace is a seascape by Monet called *Seascape at Pourville* (1882). Pourville is a town near Deauville in the northern part of France. The water you see is the English Channel, called La Manche. We have always been enchanted by this painting because of the movement of the water, as well as its apparent simplicity and marvelous perspective. We have never been able to make an exact count of the sailboats; the number changes each time we try. I feel that in this picture, Monet somehow succeeds in painting the air. Sometimes on a hot summer day, I cool off by coming in here to gaze at *Seascape at Pourville*.

In the opposite corner is a painting done in 1913 by Gino Severini, one of the Italian Futurists. That year would have been a wonderful time to have been turned loose in Paris with a checkbook, if you had the eye and the sense to buy what you were seeing.[11] Painters had come from all over Europe. Each had a different theory about painting. Some banded together and wrote manifestoes full of fierce statements. The Futurists was one of those groups whose objective was to show rapid continuous motion. Severini dedicated this painting, *Rhythm of the Dance* (1913), to his patroness, Madame Rathchilde, who had helped arrange his marriage. You can see his personal dedication and the date written at the bottom.

In the window stands the sculpture *The Age of Bronze*, finished in 1878 by Auguste Rodin. This is the work that first made his reputation. Initially, he was accused of having "sculpted from life"—molding the clay on the model, bivalving it and, after reassembling the clay halves, casting it. Rodin disproved this allegation by commissioning an extensive search for the model, who had been an Italian mercenary soldier in the Franco-Prussian war. He was brought back to Paris and testified that

---

[9]Dr. Albert Barnes' famous museum is mentioned on page 32.
[10]A very popular patented cold medicine.

[11]Four works in our collection are dated 1913: Severini's *Rhythm of the Dance*, Juan Gris' *Sheet of Music, Pipe, and Pen*, Segonzac's *Notre Dame*, and Kirchner's *Tower Room*.

Rodin had indeed modeled the piece in the true fashion.

Some books have pictures of this figure holding a staff or spear. I'm sure he was leaning on something. Just imagine being naked and holding that pose for hours in a frigid studio. Rodin later removed the staff to improve the space on that side of the body, thereby enhancing the lines of the torso. There is no question in my mind that its removal strengthened the work.

If you want to touch *The Age of Bronze*, please do. I never can resist. You can actually feel Rodin's finger-prints. This was one of the first five of the half-life-size versions of this cast, and so you know that Rodin supervised its completion.

The last work in the dining room is this little Juan Gris, *Sheet of Music, Pipe, and Pen* (1913) collage with wallpaper. In the Columbus Museum collection is a Gris of the same year that is so similar they could be brothers.

Why don't we move into the living room, where we can have our "dessert"?

" Sometimes on a hot summer day, I cool off by coming in here to gaze at Seascape at Pourville."

The Dining Room
View of Bennecourt by Monet (our first Impressionist painting)
Melanie, The Schoolteacher by Soutine

The Dining Room

(Left Corner)	*The Gypsy Girl* by Renoir
	Seascape at Pourville by Monet
(Right Corner)	*Rhythm of the Dance (Dancer)* by Severini
	The Age of Bronze by Rodin
	Assia by Despiau

The Dining Room
Rythym of the Dance by Severini

The Dining Room
Sheet of Music, Pipe, and Pen by Gris

The
Living Room

When I issued that invitation, I was thinking of an anecdote Sam Salz used to recount. In the early '30s, he, Bonnard, and several other painters used to dine together at a favorite Parisian café. One evening after dinner, Bonnard invited them all back to his studio for dessert. He seated his guests on chairs in front of his easel and pulled away a cloth to reveal a painting. There before them was a beautiful still life by Cézanne that Bonnard had just bought. "Here, my friends," said Bonnard, "is dessert."

Let's look at our second mystery painting in the collection. Well, who do you think painted that? There's usually a long pause after we ask that question. The answer is Degas. The reason even those who know their art are stumped is that he painted very few landscapes in oil. Some scholars have said that this may be Degas' only large completed, pure landscape. It's called *Houses at the Foot of a Cliff* (ca. 1895-1898), done in Normandy. The colors and the design derive from his memory. Degas was not an outdoor painter. He would take the train to Saint-Valéry-sur-Somme and stalk around the cliffs and among the houses. Then he would return to his studio, where he would paint from memory and sketches.

The next painting is a pastel by Degas called *Seated Dancer*, one of two paintings that we bought at auction.[12] Degas has given a benign treatment to this dancer. She is relaxed, compared to most of his dancers, who usually are shown in contorted postures. Supposedly, Degas was not very fond of women. He liked to show them in awkward positions in order to depict various angles of the body. This pastel was found in his studio after he died.

This little gouache by Pissarro is called *The Marketplace at Pontoise* (1887). It was a work Pissarro wrote about in his letters to his son Lucien. You should read Pissarro's letters. He could be very humorous—sometimes without meaning to be—because he felt things so deeply, often becoming angry and expressing strong opinions. *"I went to Pontoise today and I started two gouaches,"* he noted. *"One is of the marketplace."* Then a few days later, he wrote,

"The one at the marketplace is coming along, it's assez bien" (good enough).

The painting over the fireplace is, of course, by Monet. It depicts an estuary on the Seine. Called *Le Seine at Porte-Villez* (*A Gust of Wind*), 1883, this was said to be one of Monet's favorite paintings, and he kept it in his studio. A lot of people tried to buy it from him. But he turned all of them down until 1920, when he sold it to his friend Sacha Guitry, who was an actor in the Comédie Française, and about to marry the actress Yvonne Printemps. On the back of the painting it says in Monet's shaky hand: *"À Mon ami Sacha,"* [signed] *Claude Monet, 1920.*

Sam Salz used to visit Sacha and his wife in their apartment in Paris. Sam would sit there and eye this painting. Sacha finally said, "Listen, Sam, forget it. As long as I live, you are not going to buy this painting from me." Many years later, Sacha died. Sam bought the painting and then sold it to us. It is an intriguing chain of events: The painting that was created on the Seine 100 years ago came to reside in Columbus, Ohio.

To the right of the fireplace is a Pissarro of 1878, *Landscape Near Pontoise*. If you recall in the library, you saw the little Cézanne, which was done about the same time. It's possible the two artists were in Pontoise painting together. Cézanne was in Paris at the time and referred to Pissarro as "Le Maître." Pissarro had a good relationship with Cézanne, as he did with all the artists. They loved him and also called him "Le Maître." Pissarro's *Landscape Near Pontoise*, Cézanne's *Seated Bather*, Rodin's *The Age of Bronze*, and Renoir's *The Gypsy Girl* are the four earliest works in our collection.

At the end of the room, on the left, is Pissarro's *The Stone Bridge and Barges at Rouen*, done five years later in 1883. As you can see, he'd become interested in pointillism.[13] The painting

---

[12]The other one is the de Staël.
[13]A method of painting in which a white ground is systematically covered with tiny points of pure color that blend together when seen from a distance, thus producing a luminous effect.

The Living Room
Church Square, Montmagny by Utrillo
Weeping Willow by Monet
Houses at the Foot of a Cliff by Degas*
*2nd mystery painting. Refer to the "Living Room" chapter.

The Living Room
The Marketplace at Pontoise by Pissarro
The Seine at Port-Villez (A Gust of Wind) by Monet
Landscape Near Pontoise by Pissarro
The Stone Bridge and Barges at Rouen by Pissarro

reminds us that the Impressionists were artists of their time and proud of the industrial revolution. With his muted palette and the use of slender factory chimneys, Pissarro has created a seemingly serene scene on the other side of the river. In looking at this painting, the last thing you think about is factory chimneys because the overall effect is one of dreamy quietness.

Sam, referring to what he called "a typical French grey sky," said that Pissarro could paint it better than any of the Impressionists, which was ironic in that Pissarro was from St. Thomas, West Indies.

At the end of the living room is a head in bronze by Charles Despiau, a French sculptor, who died in 1946. Until now, he has not enjoyed the fame that his talent deserves. Despiau was one of Rodin's chief assistants. The bust, a portrait of a woman named Mademoiselle Giséle Gérard, was done in 1943.

Let's look now at a Fauve painting by Derain, *Portrait of the Painter Étienne Terrus* (1905). The Fauve movement started in 1905 and ended abruptly a year and a half later. It included a large group of enthusiastic young painters who were influenced by Gauguin and Van Gogh. Among the best-known Fauve painters are Derain, Matisse, Vlaminck, and Braque.

In his painting of Terrus, who was considered one of the father figures of the Fauve movement, Derain displays the typical Fauve technique. He exposes a lot of canvas, using big brush strokes and intense color.

After Terrus died, the painting passed on to his daughter, Madame Comte. Every summer Sam would call on her. He said the only reason he did was because of this wonderful Fauve portrait of her father which hung over the fireplace. During these awkward visits, Madame Comte would always serve Sam the same thing—a glass of very bad brandy. Evidently, this ceremony continued for many years: Sam would come to call, be served the bad brandy, and have a polite conversation about her father. Nothing was ever said about the portrait, and Sam would leave.

"I was getting older," Sam said, "but she was getting older than I was." Finally she got very old.

" Madame Comte would always serve Sam the same thing— a glass of very bad brandy."

Sam continued, "One day, as I was sitting there drinking the very bad brandy, she said, 'Mr. Salz, I think you want to buy the portrait of my father.' Now, you understand, this is the first time over the years that it had ever been mentioned."

Sam nodded his head politely and replied, "Yes, Madame, I would." They made whatever deal they made, and Sam left with the *Portrait of Étienne Terrus*.

Catty-corner to the Derain is the Sisley, *Boatyard at Saint-Mammés* (1885). Alfred Sisley (who was half-English, half-French) was a great friend of Monet, Pissarro, and Renoir. For years, they exhibited together. Sisley, who died when he was fifty, was the only one of the Impressionists who didn't live long enough to enjoy any kind of financial success. He was always very poor. At the time of this painting, he was writing letters such as this to his dealer: *"Mon cher Monsieur Durand Ruel. I'm sending you some canvases today. Could you please send me enough money to pay my butcher bill and baker bill..."*

The first time Howard and I saw this painting at Sam's, I thought it could be a Parisian Van Gogh. It is so vivid, so full of fire.

Next, let's look at the paintings over the couch. I always remember our excitement the night we finally were able to hang the three pictures together on this wall. Because so many groups of students have toured our home, it has occurred to me that these three paintings would make a great assignment for a paper. I should write it myself, but I'll probably never do it. You have three young women absorbed in what they are doing. They're not paying attention to any of us. You could contrast them, as well as the chairs and the backgrounds. And, of course, you could discuss the relationship among the three artists and the time that each painting was done. However, it's undoubtedly more fun to enjoy the pictures than to worry about writing a paper.

The first one is *The Breakfast (Le Petit Déjeuner)* by Degas. There's so much to discuss about this painting that even I, who enjoy talking, am compelled to fall silent in front of it. It overwhelms me. It's a perfect work of art. Our darling Sam used to say that he believed there were certain times when God's hand rested on the painter's hand. I have always felt that this work was the result of one of those instances.

But I can't remain silent. Because it's such a beautiful work, I have to emphasize some of the things Degas has accomplished in this picture.

As you look at the dancer enjoying her morning cup of coffee, take time to notice the way the chair thrusts backward and her body leans forward, creating a V-shape, which is repeated in the angle of her elbow. Look at the curves brought in by the towel across her body and the sweeps of her soft hair, as well as by that wonderful red plate. Then look at the bathtub with the grey undulating curves in the background. If you study Degas, you know that he loved that bathtub. He actually kept it in the studio and used it in a number of his paintings.

Sam told us how he happened to buy *Le Petit Déjeuner*. In 1969, it still belonged to Charles Durand-Ruel, who was then the patriarch of the family. A very tall, elegant, handsome man, he was a great friend of Sam's. At Christmas time, Sam was in Paris staying at the Plaza Athénée, and he came down with the flu. Sam had a tendency to become depressed at times. When he was sick, he was *really* depressed. Every day, Charles Durand-Ruel would call on him, very upset to see Sam so unhappy.

One day he said, "Sam, Sam, I can't stand seeing you this way. What can I do to make you happy, to make you smile again?"

Sam, gasping pathetically, said, "Oh, just bring me the little Degas for a while, and let me look at her. Then I will feel better."

I should preface this by saying that *Le Petit Déjeuner* had been in Charles Durand-Ruel's possession as long as both of them could re-

The Living Room
The Portrait of the Painter Étienne Terrus by Derain
Boatyard at Saint-Mammés by Sisley
Shelves of Etruscan Pottery
Paintings by Degas, Renoir, and Vuillard

The Living Room
The Breakfast (La Petit Déjeuner) by Degas
Christine Lerolle Embroidering by Renoir
Nude Seated before a Fireplace by Vuillard

member. Many times, Sam had hinted, to no avail, that he wanted to buy it from him. Charles, wanting to help his poor friend Sam, went home, took *Le Petit Déjeuner* off the wall, and brought it back to the Plaza Athénée. Sam took her to bed with him. He put his arms around her. While he ate his breakfast the next morning, he propped her up on the table. After breakfast, he carried her over to a chair and just sat with her on his lap. Slowly, he began to recover. You can imagine the end of the story. Charles never got the painting back. Later, we got our hands on it. And now, of course, *Le Petit Déjeuner* will be in the museum's hands.

So many people over the years have asked me to name my favorite painting and Howard's favorite painting.[14] My answer has always been that I don't have one. I really love them all. But, I say, if there were ever a fire, I'd go immediately to the living room and take down this painting, *Le Petit Déjeuner*. Then I would go for the little Vuillard, then the little Pissarro, *The Marketplace at Pontoise*. And after a quick stop in the library for the Monet *Grapes*, I'd dash upstairs for some of the Klees. In other words, I would grab only what I could carry out and, undoubtedly, be asphyxiated in the attempt.

In the center of the wall is Renoir's *Christine Lerolle Embroidering* (ca. 1895-1989). Christine Lerolle was the daughter of the Lerolle family, who were collectors. In the background are two gentlemen looking at some of the collection. The man farthest away from us is Henri Rouart, a connoisseur of the arts, an amateur painter, and a great friend of the Renoirs, Degas, and the Lerolles. One of his sons married Christine; another son married her sister.

The other man is named Devillez. He and Rouart are studying two Renoirs and a Degas. *Christine Lerolle Embroidering* reflects the comfortable bourgeois family scene that Renoir loved so much.

To the right of the Renoir is our third young woman, painted by Édouard Vuillard in his studio, around

---

[14]Howard's answer: "One night Sam and I were having a conversation in which the subject came around to a comparison of some of the Impressionist painters. I admitted how much I admired and loved Degas, and that I thought he was a masterful artist and great draftsman. But I had to insist that one of the artists I'd always loved best—and I could never really explain it—was Claude Monet. I said, 'Sam, I don't really understand it, but for me, there's something about Monet that I love.' And he said, 'Well, it's all very simple, Howard. It's just that he touches you.'"

" Sam used to say that he believed there were certain times when God's hand rested on the painter's hand."

1899. She's *Nude Seated before a Fireplace*, and Vuillard captured her sitting there, resting between poses.

Sam was a great friend of Vuillard's and had often been in his studio. He remembered the black marble fireplace and the big green portfolio. Something about this painting has always fascinated me. If you mentally exclude her figure and look at the background, you'll see that it's really a study in abstraction. The fireplace, the portfolio, the paintings on the walls—even the door to the studio—all are squares that play off against one another.

Since it's getting late and I know you'll want to have time for questions, I'm simply going to identify this second-to-last painting: *Church Square, Montmagny* (ca. 1908), by Utrillo. This was the other painting we bought that first weekend we met Sam.

This last painting, *Weeping Willow*, was our swan song. Fittingly, Howard and I acquired it through Sam, and it joined our collection in 1977. As you may already have guessed, it's by Monet, and it was painted in Giverny in 1918. Although it's a "late" Monet, he lived eight more years, during which time he did a lot of his great water-lily paintings and many other works. You can see that this painting is really Expressionism, not Impressionism. It

just seems to drip down the canvas. Somehow, Monet manages to get inside nature. On summer days, we would open the french doors, and I would say, "Now we have three great paintings on this wall: the Monet, the Degas...and nature."

The dealers Durand-Ruel and Bernheim Jeune jointly bought *Weeping Willow* (*Saule pleureur*) in 1918. A year later, they sold it to Henri Canonne, who was head of a large Swiss pharmaceutical company. He died in 1976, and Sam bought *Weeping Willow* from the estate.

One day in 1977, Sam and his wife Jan, invited us to lunch. Lunches at Sam's were always a treat. His beautiful dining room usually displayed Segonzac still lifes. Only every once in a while would there be other paintings. This day, we arrived just in time for lunch. Sam and I walked into the dining room, and, as usual, I was seated on his right. Just as I started to sit down, I had the feeling Sam was watching me. Howard was still in the hall talking to Jan. Suddenly, I sensed a tremendous presence in the room. I looked up to my left. There, hanging on the wall, was *Weeping Willow*. I was so overcome by my first sight of this painting that I started to cry. I thought it was so beautiful. I'd never seen anything like it—the power of it, the glory of it, the beauty of it.

Howard walked in, still talking to Jan. He stopped. His head snapped back. He was looking at *Weeping Willow*. "Oh, my God, oh, my God, oh, my God," was all he could say, and he started gulping down his wine. When we finally sat down, neither one of us said a word. Howard kept gulping wine, and Sam's butler kept refilling his glass. I was dabbing at my eyes and probably gulping wine, too. We kept staring at this painting.

Finally Sam laughed. "Well, you're a great pair of luncheon guests," he joked. "This is going to be interesting. We haven't heard a word out of you."

Eventually, I stopped crying, and Howard, I hope, stopped drinking wine. Together we said, "Oh, Sam, we just have to have this painting."

As it turned out, everybody that Sam knew, all those eager customers, wanted the painting, too. For what seemed like a long time, we didn't know whether we could get it. We only knew how much we loved that painting. Finally, we were *allowed* to buy *Weeping Willow*. What a glorious moment when we knew it was to be ours!

When it came into our home, Howard, with the help of Jack Greaves, worked two days moving the paintings around the house. Then suddenly the walls were filled, everything had found its place, and Howard and I agreed that we had finished our collection.

" Suddenly, I sensed a tremendous presence in the room."

Living With Art

Think of tidying up after a dinner party,
realigning the Rodin some guest left rotated
toward the garden, his glance skimming the courtyard,

straightening frames that hold Monets
dusting finger prints from a bronze bust—
("This is not a museum," she told us, "You may touch")

replacing flowers in a hall vase
fresh as the van Dongen lilacs rising behind them,
spending all Saturday trying to find
space enough for the Jawlensky.

Think of needing, all those years,
only two lamps in the vast living room,
so much light poured from above the paintings.

When leaving for the evening
think of growing accustomed to turning
on the one above your smaller Derain

as a night light.

—Karen Updike

Portrait of Maud Walter by Derain

Questions and Answers

After the tour, there was usually time for informal discussion. The following interview between Kirsten Chapman and myself reflects the most frequently asked questions.

K: *Why was Monet's* WeepingWillow *the last painting that you bought?*

B: By the time we had hung *Weeping Willow*, we suddenly realized that our house, which had always accepted more paintings, was finally full. Besides, we really couldn't afford our taste anymore. Anytime I said that on a tour, people laughed, but I really meant it. The art market in 1977-78 had taken off. We didn't want to buy works of lesser quality, and, as a matter of fact, our purchasing had decreased greatly during the '70s. The art market was going out of sight.

K: *After buying* WeepingWillow, *was there a sense of sadness knowing that you had completed the collection?*

B: No, I don't think so. I don't think we were sad. We were so excited about finally owning Monet's *Weeping Willow* and having the living room so perfectly complete. Because of the rehanging, we were able to turn our bedroom into a German Expressionist room. It looked wonderful. In the earlier years, it was a hodgepodge of paintings that wouldn't fit anywhere else. After those two days of rehanging in 1977, the paintings remained the way you see them today.

K: *Did Sam Salz ever see them this way?*

B: No, but some years ago, we finally persuaded him to come to Columbus. He was a typical New Yorker in that he thought of the United States in terms of New York on the East Coast and Los Angeles on the West Coast, with a giant wasteland in between. He cared about us, but the idea of coming to Columbus absolutely threw him. One day, we sent him a ticket so that he couldn't refuse our invitation. When Sam stepped off the plane, he was carrying a copy of *War and Peace* under his arm. He had read it before, but he said he thought that on the way out here he would have a chance to reread it. He hadn't believed me when I told him that it was a short flight.

The second time he visited, he came with his wife Jan. At that point, we had several German Expressionist paintings hanging downstairs. Although he never said so, Sam disliked having them there with "his" French Impressionists. We think he plotted to drive all the German paintings upstairs so the French paintings could take over the downstairs. This might have influenced Sam's "allowing" us to buy so many of his beautiful pictures.

K: *Did Sam Salz and Ulfert Wilke act as your advisers?*

B: This is an assumption frequently made because collectors often use advisers. Both Sam and Ulfert were very important to us, but the fact remains that Howard and I never had any advisers except ourselves. It was our avid studying of art books and art works in museums, galleries, and private collections that guided us in our choices. We were self-starters. Early on, when we saw a painting we might buy, we immediately started studying that artist. We had an insatiable curiosity.

K: *What made you and Howard decide to let the paintings go to the museum?*

B: We considered selling two or three of the paintings because we have a big family and many obligations. But, when we tried to choose which paintings to sell, Howard and I just couldn't do it. We couldn't accept having the collection dispersed. The collection we had brought together had become a very special entity. We wanted it to remain intact forever.

You'll remember that earlier on the tour I talked about how affected I was when I read that John Quinn's collection had been sold at auction after his death. We didn't want that to happen to our paintings. What would we have accomplished with our collecting, had we done that? We thought it would be wonderful if somehow, someday, the collection could remain in our community at the Columbus Museum.

It happened that on a beautiful summer day in 1981, Budd Bishop, then director of the Columbus Museum, called to ask if he could stop by. I remember our being on the porch and Budd's asking us if the museum could dare to hope that someday it might receive our collection. That started two years of conversations between us and the museum, and eventually lawyers and accountants. Finally, it was agreed that we would sell our collection to the museum at a greatly discounted price.

K: *I understand the whole collection is going to the museum. How many works does that include?*

B: Seventy-eight in all, of which seventy-four are paintings or works on paper, plus four sculptures.

K: *Can you remember how you felt that day after Budd Bishop left?*

B: Not exactly. But Howard and I felt good about the idea. Over the years, we had become more and more conscious of the large responsibility of having these great works in our home. We grew to feel we were only temporary custodians of the paintings. They have a life of their own. The museum won't totally possess them any more than we have. The most anyone can hope to be is the guardian, responsible for keeping them safe, the way parents are with children.

K: *Your words remind me of two things. One is the statement by Kahlil Gibran in which he says your children are not your children. They are the sons and daughters of life longing for itself. For, as you said, you don't own the paintings, and neither will the museum. They belong to life, and it was life longing for itself that caused them to be painted.*

The other thing I was wondering—if you had known when you bought your first painting that eventually it and all the others would be passing through your hands, do you think you would have done what you

" We thought it would be wonderful if somehow, someday, the collection could remain in our community at the Columbus Museum."

did? In other words, if you had the chance to do it all over again, would you?

B: I don't know. I really don't know. In the beginning, we obviously had the desire to acquire them because collectors are people who have the need to possess. So perhaps, had we known that we weren't going to keep them throughout our lives, then maybe we wouldn't have collected. But at that stage, we weren't thinking about the future. A kind of fever comes over collectors. I can recognize it in other people. First there's the learning, then the search, and the chase to find what you want, and then possession. Somehow, Kirsten, it makes me think of that phrase "Better to have loved and lost than never to have loved at all."

K: *Living with these great works of art must have increased your sensitivity to beauty, not just in art, but in all the arts and in all forms of nature. Have there been any other benefits that you hadn't expected?*

B: Yes. Because we studied the artists so intensively, they've become familiar personalities to us. It's as though they live here, too. There's a kind of coziness in the house, and we're part of the gang. Howard and I often say, "Wouldn't it be wonderful if they could all come to dinner?"

K: *Knowing that the paintings are going to be leaving soon, how have you been preparing to let go?*

B: I must confess the letting-go part has been extremely difficult for me. Starting three years ago, I realized that, if you take 1988 and add three to it, you suddenly have 1991. On each New Year's Eve when I got through celebrating and kissing various people's husbands, and then my own, I'd think, "Oh, my God, it's a year closer!" So I did go through a hard time because we had lived so intimately with our collection.

We never took the paintings for granted. People ask if I ever walk downstairs without looking at them. The answer is no, never! I don't mean that each time I walk down the stairs, I stop and study each painting, but they are always there for me. They've become almost like living things. I remember being in the living room one night, about six months ago. I went around touching all the paintings, saying, "I'm glad that you don't know that we're going to let you go." Howard tried to help me get through this sad time, saying, "Babs, you know they're inanimate objects, and you certainly aren't going to let inanimate objects ruin the rest of your life." I realized that he was absolutely right.

Actually I've gone through a lengthy mourning period. Probably, in the long run, it will have turned out to be a healthy thing. The museum staff has been out often to look at the works that will need restoring. This morning, in fact, professionals were photographing not only Howard and myself, but also the paintings as they appear in our home—recording for posterity. All of this has made parting with the art much more of a reality. The transfer has begun. I realize now that this is the end of a chapter. We're going to go ahead with our life in a different way.

K: *You must have had so many exhilarating experiences with the collection. Do any stand out above the others?*

B: There were so many heady days and nights that it's difficult to single out any one. But a certain morning does come to mind. Do you remember the play *Our Town* by Thornton Wilder? In the last scene, Emily dies in childbirth and goes to sit on a hill, where other dead people are waiting. They don't exactly know what they are waiting for, but they wait there. Emily is allowed to relive a day in her life, and she chooses her twelfth birthday.

In 1975, the Chicago Art Institute had a Monet show. We lent two of our paintings to the exhibit: *The Seine at Port-Villez* and *Basket of Grapes*. As lenders, we were invited to a dinner the night before the show opened to the public. It was an elegant evening. But the greatest experience—and the one I would choose to go back to—came the next morning when Howard, Ulfert, and I were permitted to view the exhibit all by ourselves. Not until 11:00 would the doors be opened to the public. We had two hours to view the 121 Monets that had been lent from all over the world.

We walked very slowly through the entire exhibition. There I was, with two men I adored. The three of us were in awe of this display of Monet's genius. His life unfolded before our eyes. We became more and more aware of his ceaseless, passionate search to perfect his vision. He was constantly, subtly changing.

As we made our way through the hushed hall, everything was like a dream. Suddenly, the two hours had passed. We left, and the doors were open to the public. Later we learned that the attendance that opening day was 7,000 people.

Unlike Emily, who was allowed only one chance to return, I've been able to remember that scene again and again. There we are—Ulfert, Howard, and I—gliding through the sunlit gallery, experiencing together one of the greatest pleasures we ever could have imagined.

" The paintings belong to life, and it was life longing for itself that caused them to be painted."

Legacy

The Living Room
Howard and I
January, 1991

"From the time of the purchase of our first painting and through all the years of buying pictures, we worked very hard to improve our 'eyes' so that we could confidently differentiate the various levels of quality. Whenever we traveled, whether in the United States or Europe, we spent most of our time visiting museums, churches (especially in Italy), or private collections. One of the great satisfactions came from the fine-tuning of our taste and seeing this become recognized by dealers and the various other art people whom we encountered. We developed faith in our collective 'eye,' and thus we would be satisfied with only the best examples of an artist's work. We were never tempted to buy just for the name. We had become, as Sam Salz put it, *collectionneurs sérieux*.

"For many years, we have lived surrounded by these great and powerful works of art. We have felt a tremendous sense of responsibility for their well-being as well as a sense of obligation to the artists themselves. We believe that these works are meant to be seen and shared with others—not just with family and friends but with the whole community—and thus for years, we opened our home to people from far and near who wished to view the art. Moreover, we recognize that these great paintings have a life of their own—they existed long before they became a part of our home and our life, and with tender and proper care, they would exist for centuries more. Thus, even though they had become part of us, we knew that we were only their temporary custodians. We wanted them always to be together in our city, Columbus, and for this reason, the arrangement was made with the Columbus Museum of Art, to ensure that generations to come would enjoy this great art.

"We hope that those who experience 'our' paintings in the museum will, as we did, receive from their beauty and their various personal messages about life some moments of joy and peace and an appreciation of man's great creative genius and its enduring spirit, which somehow enable us all to survive the worst."[15]

—*Howard and Babette Sirak*
January 24, 1991

"We knew that we were only the paintings' temporary custodians."

---

[15]*Legacy* is a quotation from the collectors' statement in the catalogue *Impressionism and European Modernism: The Sirak Collection.*

Afterword

Though family and friends urged me to write my book, the task lay in wait over a long and busy time. Then six years ago, I met Kirsten Chapman. We began a conversation that led to the creation of this book.

The story had been inside me all along, but Kirsten helped me find it and get it down on paper. Her increasing persistence and encouragement, especially during the past two years, convincing me it could be done. When I became stuck, she helped give form to what I was attempting to say. Time and again, as we sat side by side, writing and rewriting, I knew this book was truly a joint effort. Neither of us could have done it alone.

—Babs Sirak

We wrote Babs' book to preserve the intimacy and tone of her tours in the house on Commonwealth. Here, rooms were not roped off; life pulsated within. A tennis racquet might be found below van Dongen's burst of lilacs in the front hall or a grandson's Tonka truck beneath Renoir's *Christine* in the living room. Babs encouraged you to sit on the bed in the master bedroom, the better to view the Feininger and the Nolde. In the dining room, she urged you to touch Rodin's statue to find his fingerprints.

My visits with Babs, along with her interviews by several Sirak docents and some of her tours recorded by Stewart Curtis, became the rich fabric of her manuscript. But it is Babs and Howard who have woven the richest tapestry, their love affair—the Sirak Collection.

—Kirsten Chapman

The Sirak Collection

Max Beckmann
German, 1884–1950
Two Negroes in a Cabaret   91.1.1
Zwei Neger im Varieté
1946
Oil on canvas, 27 $^{11}/_{16}$ x 20 $^{1}/_{8}$ in.
   (70.3 x 51.1 cm.)
Signed and incorrectly dated lower right:
   Beckmann 47

Julius Bissier
German, 1893–1965
usque ad finem   91.1.3
1961
Brush and watercolor on off-white paper,
   5 $^{7}/_{8}$ x 9 $^{1}/_{2}$ in. (14.9 x 24.1 cm.)
Inscribed, dated, and signed lower right:
   Rondine 9.11.61.x./Jules Bissier
Inscribed upper left: usque ad finem.

Julius Bissier
A.31.Oct.62   91.1.2
1962
Watercolor on linen, 8 $^{5}/_{8}$ x 9 $^{13}/_{16}$ in.
   (22 x 25.1 cm.)
Inscribed and signed lower left:
   A.31.Oct.62/Jules Bissier

Pierre Bonnard
French, 1867–1947
Portrait of Thadée Natanson   91.1.4
1897
Oil on board, 17 x 16 $^{1}/_{2}$ in. (43.1 x 41.9 cm.)
Inscribed and dated lower left: Bonnard à
   Thadée Souvenir de l'été 97

Paul Cézanne
French, 1839–1906
Seated Bather   91.1.5
Baigneuse assise
ca. 1873-1877
Oil on canvas, 8 $^{1}/_{4}$ x 5 $^{1}/_{8}$ in. (21 x 13 cm.)

Edgar Degas
French, 1834–1917
The Breakfast   91.1.8
Le Petit Déjeuner
ca. 1885
Pastel and graphite over monotype on cream
   paper, laid down, image size: 15 $^{5}/_{16}$ x 11 $^{7}/_{16}$
   in. (38.7 x 29 cm.); mount size: 17 $^{5}/_{8}$ x 13 $^{7}/_{8}$
   in. (44.8 x 34.5 cm.)
Signed upper right: Degas

Edgar Degas
Houses at the Foot of a Cliff   91.1.7
Maisons au pied d'une falaise
   (Saint-Valéry-sur-Somme)
ca. 1895–1898
Oil on canvas, 36 $^{1}/_{4}$ x 28 $^{5}/_{8}$ in. (92 x 73.2 cm.)
Stamped lower left: Degas

Edgar Degas
Seated Dancer   91.1.6
Danseuse assise
ca. 1898
Pastel and charcoal on tan paper, laid down,
   21 x 19 $^{7}/_{16}$ in. (53.2 x 49.4 cm.)
Stamped, lower left: Degas

Robert Delaunay
French, 1885–1941
Portuguese Woman   91.1.10
Portugaise
1916
Oil on canvas, 53 $^{1}/_{2}$ x 61 $^{3}/_{8}$ in.
   (135.9 x 155.8 cm.)
Signed lower right: r. delaunay 1916

Robert Delaunay
*Air, Iron, and Water (study for the mural in
   the Pavillon des Chemins de Fer, Exposition
   International, Paris, 1937)*   91.1.9
Air, fer et eau
1936–1937
Casein on paper, mounted on canvas (in 1951),
   38 $^{7}/_{16}$ x 59 $^{7}/_{16}$ in. (97.6 x 151 cm.)

André Derain
French, 1880–1954
Portrait of Maud Walter   91.1.12
ca. 1904-1906
Oil on board (cradled), 14 ⅞ x 10 ½ in.
   (37.7 x 26.6 cm.)

André Derain
Portrait of the Painter Étienne Terrus   91.1.11
1905
Oil on canvas, 25 ¾ x 19 ½ in.
   (65.4 x 49.5 cm.)
Signed lower left: A. Derain

Charles Despiau
French, 1874–1946
Mademoiselle Gisèle Gérard   91.1.13
1942–1943
Bronze, H. 17 ¾ in. (45.1 cm.)
Signed on verso and inscribed: C. Despiau,
   Valsuani, Paris 5/10

James Ensor
Belgian, 1860–1949
The Assassination   91.1.14
L'Assassinat
1890
Oil on canvas, 23 ¹³/₁₆ x 30 ⅜ in.
   (60.5 x 77 cm.)
Signed and dated lower right: Ensor 90

James Ensor
The Sea Shells   91.1.15
Les Coquillages
1895
Oil on canvas, 32 ⁵/₁₆ x 43 in. (82.2 x 109.2 cm.)
Signed and dated lower right: ENSOR 1895
   J. Ensor [painted over, indistinct]

Lyonel Feininger
American, 1871–1956
Cathedral   91.1.16
Der Dom
1920
Oil on canvas, 35 ⅝ x 45 ¼ in.
   (90.5 x 114.9 cm.)
Signed and dated lower right: Feininger 20

Lyonel Feininger
Ship in Distress   91.1.17
1946
Watercolor on light tan paper, 9 ½ x 11 ⅜ in.
   (24.2 x 28.9 cm.)
Signed, inscribed, and dated: Feininger Ship
   in Distress 18. x. 46

Albert Gleizes
French, 1881–1953
To Jacques Nayral   91.1.18
À Jacques Nayral
1917
Oil on board, 29 ⅞ x 23 ⅝ in. (75.9 x 60 cm.)
Signed and dated lower right: Alb Gleizes 17.
   Inscribed lower right: à jacques nayral

Juan Gris
Spanish, 1887–1927
Sheet of Music, Pipe, and Pen   91.1.19
Musique, plume et pipe
1913
Oil and collage on canvas, 10 ¾ x 13 ⅝ in.
   (27.3 x 35.2 cm.)
Signed and dated on verso: Juan Gris 5-13

Alexej Jawlensky
Russian, 1864–1941
Schokko with Red Hat   91.1.20
Schokko mit Rotem Hut
1909[?] or 1910
Oil on board, 29 ¾ x 25 ⅞ in.
   (74.7 x 65.7 cm.)
Signed and dated lower left: A. Jawlensky
   190[?]

Ernst Ludwig Kirchner
German, 1880–1938
Girl Asleep   91.1.22
Schlafendes Mädchen
1905–1906
Oil on board, 20 ⅜ x 17 ⅛ in.
   (51.9 x 43.5 cm.)
Signed lower right and incorrectly dated: E.L.
   Kirchner 1901. Signed lower left (scratched):
   ELK

Ernst Ludwig Kirchner
Landscape at Fehmarn with Nudes
    (Five Bathers at Fehmarn)   91.1.21
Fehmarnlandschaft mit Akte
    (Fünf Badende auf Fehmarn)
1913
Oil on canvas, 47 ⁷/₈ x 35 ³/₄ in.
    (121.6 x 90.8 cm.)
Signed lower right with monogram (indistinct).
    Inscribed on verso: E.L. Kirchner

Ernst Ludwig Kirchner
Tower Room, Fehmarn
    (Self-Portrait with Erna)   91.1.23
Turmzimmer, Fehmarn (Selbstbildnis mit Erna)
1913
Oil on canvas, 36 x 32 ¹/₄ in. (91.4 x 81.9 cm.)
    Signed lower right: E.L. Kirchner. Signed,
    dated, and inscribed on verso: E.L.
    Kirchner/1913/Turmzimmer

Paul Klee
Swiss, 1879–1940
View of Saint Germain   91.1.33
Ansicht von Saint Germain
1914
Watercolor on tan paper, laid down,
    9 x 11 ¹/₈ in. (23 x 28.4 cm.)
Signed upper left: Klee. Dated and inscribed
    at bottom: 1914.41.Ansicht v. St. Germain.

Paul Klee
With the Yellow Half-moon
    and Blue Star   91.1.34
Mit dem gelben Halbmond und blauen Stern
1917
Watercolor on paper, laid down,
    7 ⁵/₈ x 5 ⁵/₈ in. (19.5 x 14.3 cm.)
Signed lower left: Klee. Dated and inscribed
    at bottom: 1917/51. Inscribed lower
    right corner: A.K.18.

Paul Klee
City between Realms   91.1.30
Stadt im Zwischenreich
1921
Transfer print with black ink and watercolor
    on paper, laid down, 12 ¹/₄ x 18 ⁷/₈ in.
    (31.3 x 48 cm.)
Signed lower left: Klee. Dated and inscribed at
    bottom: 1921/25 Stadt im Zwischenreich

Paul Klee
Dream of a Fight   91.1.32
Traum von einem Kampf
1924
Graphite on light tan paper, laid down,
    11 ¹/₈ x 8 ⁷/₈ in. (28.2 x 22.6 cm.)
Signed, dated, and inscribed lower left:
    Klee/1924 4/12. Dated and inscribed on
    mount, bottom center: 1924 84 Traum von
    einem Kampf

Paul Klee
Thoughtful   91.1.29
Nachdenksam über Lagen
1928
Watercolor and graphite on cream paper, laid
    down, 15 ⁹/₁₆ x 8 ⁷/₈ in. (39.6 x 22.5 cm.)
Inscribed and dated lower right: Nachdenksam
    über Lagen 1927 [badly faded]. Dated and
    inscribed lower left: 1928 9n9

Paul Klee
Composition   91.1.24
1931
Encaustic on board, 21 ¹/₂ x 27 ³/₈ in.
    (54.6 x 69.3 cm.)

Paul Klee
Still Life with Dove   91.1.31
Stilleben mit der Taube
1931
Oil and encaustic on board, 22 ¹/₄ x 28 ¹/₄ in.
    (56.4 x 71.8 cm.)
Signed lower left: Klee

Paul Klee
Rock Flower   91.1.26
Felsen blume
1932
Watercolor and pen and ink on paper, laid
    down, 17 ³/₈ x 12 ³/₄ in.
    (44.4 x 32.3 cm.)
Signed upper left: Klee. Dated and inscribed:
    1932 M4 Felsen blume. Inscribed at
    bottom: M4

Paul Klee
Lonely Flower   91.1.25
Einsame Blüte
1934
Watercolor with pen and black ink on tan
    paper, laid down, 18 ⁷/₈ x 12 ³/₈ in.
    (47.8 x 31.5 cm.)
Signed lower left: Klee. Dated and inscribed
    on verso: VI 1934 5 einsame Blüte

Paul Klee
Ilfenburg   91.1.28
1935
Gouache on paper, 11 ⁷/₈ x 10 ³/₈ in.
    (30.3 x 26.2 cm.)

Paul Klee
Fire Spirit   91.1.27
Feuer-geist
1939
Gouache on paper, laid down, 13 x 8 ¹/₈ in.
    (32.9 x 20.8 cm.)
Signed upper right: Klee. Dated and inscribed
    at bottom: 1939 xx 12 Feuer-geist

Gustav Klimt
Austrian, 1862–1918
The Embrace   91.1.35
Das Liebespaar
ca. 1910
Graphite on tan paper, 20 ³/₄ x 14 ¹/₂ in.
    (52.9 x 37 cm.)
Signed lower right: Gustav Klimt

Gustav Klimt
Portrait of Adele Bloch-Bauer   91.1.36
Bildnis Adele Bloch-Bauer
1910-1911
Graphite on light cream paper,
    22 ¹/₄ x 14 ⁵/₈ in. (56.6 x 37.2 cm.)
Signed lower right: Gustav Klimt

Henri Matisse
French, 1869–1954
Still Life with Self-Portrait   91.1.38
Nature morte à l'autoportrait
1896
Oil on canvas, 25 ⁵/₈ x 31 ³/₄ in.
    (65.1 x 80.5 cm.)
Signed lower left: H. Matisse

Henri Matisse
Maternity   91.1.37
Maternité
1939
Charcoal on tan paper, 24 x 24 in.
    (60.9 x 60.9 cm.)
Signed and dated lower right:
    Henri Matisse 39

Claude Monet
French, 1840–1926
Seascape at Pourville   91.1.39
Marine à Pourville
1882
Oil on canvas, 23 ⁵/₈ x 39 ⁷/₁₆ in.
    (60 x 100.2 cm.)
Signed lower right: Claude Monet

Claude Monet
The Seine at Port-Villez
    (A Gust of Wind)   91.1.43
La Seine à Port-Villez (Le Coup de vent)
1883 or 1890
Oil on canvas, 23 ³/₄ x 39 ¹/₄ in.
    (60.3 x 99.7 cm.)
Signed and incorrectly dated lower left:
    Claude Monet 84. Inscribed on verso in
    Monet's hand: À mon ami Sacha Claude
    Monet

Claude Monet
Basket of Grapes   91.1.40
Panier de raisins
1883 or 1884
Oil on canvas (one of six panels for a door),
    20 ⅛ x 15 in. (51.2 x 38.1 cm.)
Signed upper left: Cl. Monet

Claude Monet
View of Bennecourt   91.1.42
Vue sur Bennecourt
1887
Oil on canvas, 32 ⅛ x 32 ⅛ in.
    (81.6 x 81.6 cm.)
Signed and dated lower left: Claude Monet 87

Claude Monet
Weeping Willow   91.1.41
Saule pleureur
1918
Oil on canvas, 51 ⅝ x 43 ⁷⁄₁₆ in.
    (131.2 x 110.3 cm.)
Signed and dated lower left: Claude Monet
    1918

Giorgio Morandi
Italian, 1890–1964
Still Life with Statuette   91.1.45
Natura morta con la statuina
1922
Etching on light brown paper, image size:
    2 ⅜ x 2 ⅞ in. (6 x 7.4 cm.); paper size:
    4 ¾ x 6 ½ in. (12.1 x 16.5 cm.)
Signed and dated lower right: Morandi 1922.
    Numbered lower left: 17/30

Giorgio Morandi
Still Life with Seven Objects in a Tondo 91.1.44
Natura morta con sette oggetti in un tondo
1945
Etching on light tan paper, 10 ½ x 11 ¾ in.
    (26.7 x 29.9 cm.)
Signed and dated lower right: Morandi 1945.
    Numbered lower left: 48/50. Plate
    signed and dated: Morandi, 1945

Giorgio Morandi
Still Life   91.1.46
Natura morta
1945
Oil on canvas, 15 ⅝ x 19 ⅜ in.
    (39.5 x 49.2 cm.)
Signed and dated, left of center: Morandi 1945

Jan Müller
American, born in Germany, 1922–1958
Apparition from Hamlet   91.1.47
1957
Oil on wood, 11 x 16 ⅝ in. (28 x 41.5 cm.)
Painted on verso: Abstract (Mosaic)

Emil Nolde
German, 1867–1956
Steamboat and Sailboat   91.1.48
Dampfer und Segler
1913
Watercolor on tan paper, 10 ⁷⁄₁₆ x 15 ⅞ in.
    (26.6 x 40.4 cm.)
Signed lower right: Nolde. Dated lower left:
    1913

Emil Nolde
Young Girl   91.1.50
Junges Mädchen
1920
Watercolor on paper, 18 ½ x 14 ⅛ in.
    (46.9 x 35.8 cm.)
Signed lower right: Nolde

Emil Nolde
Sunflowers in the Windstorm   91.1.49
Sonnenblumen im Sturmwind
1943
Oil on board, 28 ⅝ x 34 ⅝ in.
    (72.6 x 88.1 cm.)
Signed lower right: Emil Nolde

Camille Pissarro
French, 1830–1903
Landscape near Pontoise   91.1.52
Paysage près Pontoise
1878
Oil on canvas, 21 ¼ x 25 ⅝ in.
    (53.9 x 65.1 cm.)
Signed and dated lower right: C. Pissarro. 78

Camille Pissarro
The Stone Bridge and Barges at Rouen 91.1.53
Le Pont de pierre et les péniches à Rouen
1883
Oil on canvas, 21 3/8 x 25 5/8 in.
  (54.3 x 65.2 cm.)
Signed and dated lower right: C. Pissarro 1883

Camille Pissarro
The Marketplace at Pontoise 91.1.51
Le Marché de Pontoise
1887
Brush and black ink, with gouache and
  watercolor, heightened with white lead,
  on tan paper, laid down, (sight) 12 3/4 x
  9 3/4 in. (32.6 x 24.8 cm.)
Signed and dated lower left: C. Pissarro. 1887

Odilon Redon
French, 1840–1916
The Two Graces 91.1.54
Les Deux Grâces
ca. 1900
Oil on canvas, 16 1/2 x 11 3/8 in.
  (41.3 x 28.3 cm.)

Pierre-Auguste Renoir
French, 1841–1919
The Gypsy Girl 91.1.56
La Bohémienne
1879
Pastel on prepared canvas, 23 x 14 1/8 in.
  (58.6 x 36 cm.)
Signed lower right: Renoir

Pierre-Auguste Renoir
The Bay of Naples 91.1.55
La Baie de Naples
1882
Oil on canvas, 11 1/2 x 15 3/8 in. (29 x 38.9 cm.)
Signed and dated lower right: Renoir 82

Pierre-Auguste Renoir
Christine Lerolle Embroidering 91.1.57
Christine Lerolle brodant
ca. 1895–1898
Oil on canvas, 32 1/8 x 25 7/8 in.
  (82.6 x 65.8 cm.)
Signed lower left: Renoir

Auguste Rodin
French, 1840–1917
The Age of Bronze 91.1.58
L'Age d'airain
1875–1876
Bronze, H. 41 1/2 in. (105.4 cm.)
Signed on top of base (right): Rodin.
  Signed on side of pedestal: Alexis Rudier,
  Fondeur, Paris

Medardo Rosso
Italian, 1858–1928
Sick Boy 91.1.59
Bimbo malato
ca. 1893
Wax, H. 9 3/8 in. (23.8 cm.)

Medardo Rosso
Head of a Young Woman 91.1.60
Busto di donna
ca. 1901
Wax over plaster (unique copy), H. 15 3/4 in.
  (40 cm.)
Signed lower right: M. Rosso

Egon Schiele
Austrian, 1890–1918
The Thinker (Self-Portrait) 91.1.61
Der Denker (Selbstbildnis)
1914
Graphite on light tan paper, 19 x 12 3/4 in.
  (48.3 x 32.4 cm.)
Signed and dated lower right: Egon Schiele
  1914. Inscribed on verso: 8 x 13/Portrait ...
  [indistinct]

André Dunoyer de Segonzac
French, 1884–1974
Notre-Dame de Paris 91.1.65
1913
Oil on canvas, 28 5/8 x 39 3/8 in.
  (73.3 x 100 cm.)
Signed lower right: A. de Segonzac

André Dunoyer de Segonzac
Provençal Farm   91.1.63
Ferme Provençale
1952
Pen and brush with ink and chalk on paper,
    laid down, 15 ⁹/₁₆ x 22 ¹⁵/₁₆ in.
    (39.5 x 58.3 cm.)
Signed lower right: A. Dunoyer de Segonzac

André Dunoyer de Segonzac
The Foot of the Valley   91.1.64
Le Fond du golfe
1952
Pen and brushwith ink on off-white paper, laid
    down, 15 ¹/₂ x 23 ¹/₈ in. (39.4 x 58.7 cm.)
Signed lower right: A. Dunoyer de Segonzac

André Dunoyer de Segonzac
The Cypress by the Sea (Saint-Tropez)   91.1.66
Le Cyprès devant la mer (Saint-Tropez)
1956
Watercolor on paper, 22 ¹/₂ x 31 in.
    (57.2 x 78.8 cm.)
Signed lower right: A. Dunoyer de Segonzac.
    Inscribed on verso: Le Cyprès devant la mer

André Dunoyer de Segonzac
The Dog   91.1.62
Le Chien
Pen and brush with black ink on white paper,
    6 ⁵/₈ x 7 in. (16.8 x 17.8 cm.)
Signed at bottom: A.D. de Segonzac

Gino Severini
Italian, 1883–1966
Rhythm of the Dance (Dancer)   91.1.67
Rythme de danse (danseuse)
1913
Oil, plaster, and sequins on board,
    (sight) D. 10 ³/₄ in. (27.3 cm.)
Inscribed and signed lower left: À Madame
    Rachilde souvenir de son admirateur Gino
    Severini. Dated lower right: Paris août 1913.
    On verso: Gino Severini, Paris 1913/Rythme
    de Danse.

Alfred Sisley
French, 1839–1899
Boatyard at Saint-Mammès   91.1.68
Chantier à Saint-Mammès
1885
Oil on canvas, 21 ⁵/₈ x 28 ⁷/₈ in.
    (54.9 x 73.3 cm.)
Signed and dated lower left: Sisley 85

Chaim Soutine
Lithuanian, 1893–1943
Landscape at Céret   91.1.70
Paysage de Céret
1920–1921
Oil on canvas, 24 ¹¹/₁₆ x 32 ³/₄ in.
    (63.4 x 83.2 cm.)
Signed lower left: Soutine

Chaim Soutine
Melanie, The Schoolteacher   91.1.71
Melanie l'institutrice
ca. 1922
Oil on canvas, 32 ¹/₈ x 18 ¹/₈ in.
    (81.5 x 46 cm.)
Signed lower left: C. Soutine

Chaim Soutine
Landscape at Cagnes   91.1.69
Paysage de Cagnes
1923
Oil on canvas, 25 ³/₄ x 32 ¹/₈ in.
    (65.5 x 80.5 cm.)
Signed lower right: Soutine

Nicolas de Staël
French, born in Russia, 1914–1955
The Volume of Things   91.1.72
Volume des choses
1949
Oil on panel, 72 ¹/₄ x 39 ¹/₈ in.
    (183.6 x 99.4 cm.)
Signed lower left: Staël

Maurice Utrillo
French, 1883-1955
Church Square, Montmagny   91.1.73
Place de l'Église à Montmagny
ca. 1908
Oil on canvas, 21 ⁵/₁₆ x 28 ¹³/₁₆ in.
   (54.1 x 73.1 cm.)
Signed lower left: Maurice Utrillo v.

Kees van Dongen
Dutch, 1877–1968
Lilacs with Cup of Milk   91.1.74
Lilas et tasse de lait
1909
Oil on canvas, 44 ³/₁₆ x 36 ⁷/₈ in.
   (120.3 x 93.7 cm.)

Maria Elena Vieira da Silva
French, born in Portugal, 1908
The Atlantic   91.1.75
Atlantique
1961
Oil on canvas, 31 ³/₄ x 39 ³/₈ in.
   (80.6 x 100 cm.)
Signed and dated lower right:
   Vieira da Silva 61

Maurice de Vlaminck
French, 1876–1958
Field of Wheat   91.1.76
Champ de blé
n.d.
Oil on canvas, 10 ⁵/₈ x 13 ³/₄ in. (27 x 35 cm.)
Signed lower left: Vlaminck

Édouard Vuillard
French, 1868–1940
Nude Seated before a Fireplace   91.1.78
Nu assis devant la cheminée
ca. 1899
Oil on canvas, 13 ¹/₂ x 12 ³/₄ in.
   (34.5 x 32.2 cm.)
Signed lower right: E. Vuillard

Édouard Vuillard
The Big Tree (The Tree Trunk)   91.1.77
Le Grand Arbre (Le tronc)
ca. 1930
Charcoal and pastel on brown paper, laid
   down on canvas, 43 ¹³/₁₆ x 32 ¹/₂ in.
   (111.3 x 82.5 cm.)
Stamped lower left: E. Vuillard